A U S T R A L I A E

Australian Folklore

ILLUSTRATED

LEATHERWOOD PRESS

Contents

INTRODUCTION

CONVICTS AND SETTLERS 8

Jump Out, Isaac - Miserablest People - Wretched Sydney - Lags and Canaries - The Ring - Last of a Race - A British Object - Margaret Catchpole - The King of Iceland - A Snake Pit - Barclay's Tigers - Tolpuddle Martyrs - The Wild White Man - The Man They Couldn't Hang - Lost in Tasmania - True Patriots All - A Useful Tree -The Convicts' Lament - Botany Bay - Poetic Broadside - Dungaree Settlers - The Rum Rebellion - Jim Jones - The Transport Ships.

GOLDEN YEARS 40

The First Find - A Different Strike - Historic Legacy - A Miner's Saga - Lasseter's Lost Reef - Bobby Dazzler - Scot's Chinese - Kerr's Hundredweight - The Rebellion at Eureka - A Ballad of Eureka - The Rebel Flag - The Whip Hand.

BUSHRANGERS 24

A History of Bushranging - A Prophecy - Black Jack's Last Words - Chinese Bushranger - Govemor of the Rangers - Ballads of the Bushrangers - Dunn, Gilbert and Ben Hall - Jack Donahue.

PEOPLE AND PLACES 50

Nationalism - Antipodeans - Father of Federation - The Australian Flag - The Larrikin Pushes - Portrait of the Larrikin - Larrikin Language - Inventive Explorer - Old Bell - Strange Sounding Names - The Ruined City - Battle of Rothbury - Missing Mace - Cooee - Worst Flood - Royal Rampage - The Impressionists - A Long Line - Early Actors - High Jinks - Not To Knight - The Lagerphone - The Fish and Chips - Box Hill Messiah - Hero of the Skies - King of Bass Strait - Sing 'em Muck - A Little Heroine -

Much Married Bishop - A Tribal Ruler - The Tichborne Case - A Tragic Hero - Adam Lindsay Gordon - The Big Apple - The Flying Pieman - An Australian Heroine - Tales of Henry Lawson - Manning Clark on Lawson - Andy's Gone With Cattle - Queen of the Earth - Boozing Celebrities - In Memoriam - John Norton's Pen - Caroline Chisholm - The Little Digger - The Building Governor.

AUSTRALIAN HUMOUR 78

Humour - Mountain of Rabbits - The Austra-laise - Celebrities - Parliamentary Humour - The Menzies Touch - Humour in Court - Pig Iron Bob - Pioneer Pannikins.

BUSH WANDERERS 92

Where the Dead Men Lie - A Damper as Heavy as Lead - The Real Clancy - Clancy of the Overflow - Bullocky-Oh! - Bullocky Bill - Mateship - Such is Life - The bullockies' Ball - Cobb & Co - The Bullockies - The Overlander - Cattle Duffers - Making Do - Rough Riders - A Fearful Track - Ten, Ten, Two and Four - The Old Bark Hut - Five Miles from Gundagai - They Dying Stockman - Sundowners - The Billy.

ON THE STATION 112

The Ringer - Click Go The Shears - Bush Fires - Famous Bells - The Bangtail Muster - Cockatoos and Jackeroos - Calendar House - The Sick Stockrider - Belyando Spew - The Rabbit Arrives - Some Advice on Rabbits - Bush Expressions - Blood on the Wattle - Bowyangs - Blue Stew - Billy Tea - The Red Bull - Up Country - Brumbies - A Squatter's Castle - A Pommy Jackeroo - How to Succeed - Said Hanrahan.

THE SPORTING LIFE 136

The Great Australian Game - Tub Races - Cricket Record - Picnic Races - Betting Bowler - The Great Trumper - Rorke's Drift - The First Cricket Team was Black - The Demon - The Master - The Tragedy of Les Darcy - Bare Knuckles - Popular Cheer - The Tied Test - Old Jack - The Golden Girl -

Rules Invented - The Barracker - Long Swims - Surfing Illegal - How League Began - The Red Terror - The First Skiers - The Prince - The Greatest Day - Referee Wins - Boxing Marathon - Classic Fight - Kangaroo Rocket - Cycling Phenomenon - Amazing Golf Record - The Million Dollar Mermaid - A Nation of Swimmers - The Australian Crawl - Golf Arrives in Australia - Troop Ships - How McDougall Topped the Score.

AUSTRALIANS AT WAR 156

The First Force - Emu Feathers - The Brisbane Line - Short on Discipline - Ice Cream War - Chokkos Save Day - Furphies - Fuzzy Wuzzy's - Monash's Greatness - Army Slang - Battle of Brisbane - Arnott's Parrots - The Anzac Book - The Anzacs - Slouch Hat - Jacka, VC - Diggers - 'ANZAC' is Born - The 1ST AIF - The Western Front - The Light Horse at Gallipoli - The Navy - The RAN - Tobruk

THE UNEXPLAINED 170

Birth of the Bunyip - Ghost Stories - The Mystery of Leichhardt - Mysterious Disappearances.

ACKNOWLEDGEMENTS

Introduction

This collection of handed down stories and folk traditions, of larger-than-life Australian characters, of unusual and mysterious events and great moments in Australian history is aimed at uncovering the strands and styles of Australian life that have created our national character.

The question arises: What is folklore? Is it the tall tales, the myths and legends, stories of the macabre and the unexplained that filter through history and become entangled and embellished to a point where the source is unknown and the incidents obscured? This is certainly true folklore, and in other countries with centuries of history and layers of lost cultures behind them, it is a rich area for rewarding entertainments.

But another kind of material can stand beside the dimly remembered tales of the past and give us a greater understanding of our people and their lives. We can search our history for real characters and incidents—the heroic, dramatic, humorous or merely quaint—and record this as a slice of the multi-faceted life of a people.

And we can draw on the works of the recorders of life, now and in the past and see the Australian scene through their eyes. Who better to give his thoughts on the Australian tradition of mateship than the champion of the battler and the "bard of the bush", Henry Lawson? Who better to conjure up a vision of the rugged, open-hearted life of the drover than the great poet. A. B. "Banjo" Paterson? There have been many recorders of the Australian way of life — Marcus Clarke, Duke Sutton, Edward S. Sorenson, C. E. W. Bean, Nehemiah Bartley — even international figures like D. H. Lawrence, Mark Twain and Anthony Trollope. Their impressions and their encounters in Australia make fascinating reading, and create for the reader of today a more direct and credible link with our past than the apocryphal tales of orally based folklore, however entertaining.

This volume is directed toward being an entertaining miscellany using the modest definition of folklore. It covers many areas: from settlement days to the sporting arena; from bushranger to modern warfare. It is mostly lighthearted, but with a lot of drama and a touch of unvarnished patriotism thrown in.

Convicts & Settlers

Jump Out, Isaac

The first Englishman to land on Australian soil with Captain Cook's party on 28 April 1770, was his wife's nephew, Isaac Smith, who sailed as midshipman cook. Cook anchored in what is now Botany Bay in the Endeavour and took a party in a ship's boat to the nearest landing place. He is said to have stood up and called to Smith, "Jump out, Isaac."

Captain James Cook proclaims New South Wales a British possession at Botany Bay in 1770. The lithograph is taken from a painting by E A. Gilfillan.

Miserablest People

When Captain William Dampier arrived on Australia's north-west coast following his second voyage into Australian waters in 1699, he described the Aborigines he met there as "the miserablest people in the world". Dampier went on to say, "The Hodmanods of Monomatapa, they were nasty people, yet for wealth are gentlman to these."

Wretched Sydney

Sydney Harbour was described by Captain Arthur Phillip as the finest natural harbour in the world, but early Sydney was not a pretty place according to this letter from the wife of the wool pioneer, John Macarthur, written in 1790. " Everything was wretched— the filthy ships in the cove; the rude lines of sodden barracks; the tents that held the sick, sagging in the downpour along the water front; the night fires in the regions of the Rocks, a sink of evil already and more like a gypsy encampment than part of a town . . . the stumps of fallen trees and the boggy tracks wending their way round rock and precipice; the oozy tank stream spreading itself out over the sand by the head of the cove."

A 1793 picture by Spaniard Juan Ravenent of convicts at New Holland. The simple but compelling sketch was one of a set of drawings made on the Spanish Scientific Expedition to the Pacific.

Lags And Canaries

In convict days a lot of expressions were developed to describe certain classes of convicts, and they were used either to delineate a type of convict or a change of status. Convicts went under names like Canary, which was derived from the Old English slang for a gaol bird, a lag or (when he was freed) an old lag, a crossbred, a transport or even a felon swell — a convict whose wealth and/or aristocratic ties gained him preferment. A Sydney convict might be known as a cockatoo hand or a Cockatoo Islander, and a Hawkesbury duck would be a convict assigned for work in the Hawkesbury area. A Van Dieman's Land convict might be known as a demon and a Hobart convict, a Derwent duck. Convicts whose sentences had expired became expirees while those who were pardoned were emancipates. Free people sometimes styled themselves as Sterling as opposed to the expression Currency, which applied to convicts or Australian born people of European origin. The expressions currency lad, currency lass, currency belles, currency criminals etc, became widely used.

The Ring

It is widely known, but not proven or documented, that there existed on Norfolk Island a secret society of convicts known as The Ring. The Ring was reputed to be a staunch brotherhood of the most hardened and dangerous convicts who terrorised their timid fellows, had them do their bidding and exacted tribute from them. D. Collins in part of his Account of New South Wales written in 1798, refers to "the fraternal society of Norfolk Island" which the convicts formed among themselves. The expression The Ring is said to derive from a place on the island known as The Ring.There some of the hardened criminals were in the habit of gathering.

Last Of A Race

Truganini, the daughter of a chief of Bruny Island, was believed to have been the last of her race of Tasmanian Aborigines and she became a celebrated person before her death in 1876. She was abducted by the whites when she was young and spent most of her life with them. She helped George Robinson with his work of removing the remnants of the Tasmanian tribes to the islands in Bass Strait. A Mrs. Seymour, who died on Kangaroo Island in 1909, became acknowledged as being the last of the Tasmanian tribes which had been depleted by the administration-backed "Black War" in Tasmania, designed to bring an end to the freedom of movement of Tasmanian Aborigines. The Aborigines, who retaliated for the loss of their tribal land by attacks on the white settlers, were ruthlessly exterminated until there was only a pitiful number left to be transferred to the Bass Strait islands.

A British Object

One of a number of wild white men who lived with Aborigines was James Murrells, who was an able seaman in the ship Peruvian when it was wrecked off the coast of Queensland. Of the 21 people on board only seven reached land, and after 42 days on a raft three died within a few days and the others were captured by blacks. Murrells was the only one to survive. On various occasions he heard that boats had come ashore from passing vessels, but when the blacks did their best to notify the sailors that a white man was with them they were misunderstood. Eventually Murrells heard of the arrival of white men in the district and searched until he found a sheep yard on the Burdekin River. He hailed his occupants with, "What cheer mates. Don't shoot. I'm a British object." At the sheep herder's hut he was told that the date was 25 January 1863, so he had been with the Aborigines for 17 years. Murrells returned to his tribe and told them he was going away. He later described the scene. "The man I was living with burst into tears, so did his gin and several other gins and men: it was a wild and

Eaylehawk Neck is a narrow strip of land near Port Arthur and was a perfect trap for escaping convicts They either had to take to the sea or run the gauntlet at the Neck - past barricades patrolled by armed guards and a line of dogs chained across the isthmus.

touching scene. There was a short, sharp struggle between the love I had for my friends and companions and the desire once more to live a civilised life." Murrells was the object of great attention when he returned to civilisation. His teeth had worn down to the gums from eating rough food and he was many years in recovering his knowledge of English.

A view of the prison settlement at Port Arthur in 1859. The beautiful sandstone church and many of the settlement's buildings, were destroyed by fire The 'worst type' of male convicts were sent to Port Arthur and were kept in conditions of unmitigated severity.

Margaret Catchpole

Australia's most colourful convict woman was Margaret Catchpole, who was born in Suffolk in 1762 and became famous in her region at the age of 24 when she galloped a spirited pony bareback to Ipswich to fetch a physician for the sick wife of her father's employer. This exploit won her the position of maid servant in the family of an Ipswich brewer. Her troubles began when she fell in love with a young smuggler and stole a horse from her master's stable to ride to London, 70 miles away, in eight and a half hours. There she was caught and sentenced to seven years' imprisonment.

In 1800 she broke out of Ipswich gaol to rejoin her mother but was recaptured and sentenced to death her sentence then being commuted to one of transportation for life. She became an assigned convict in the Colonies and met a young botanist, George Caley, a protege of Joseph Banks and superintendent of Sydney's Botanical Gardens. He asked her to marry him, but she was resolved not to marry as her smuggler lover had been killed in attempting to protect her against recapture.

From 1804 she worked in the Hawkesbury district as a midwife and attended the wife of Richard Rouse who later moved with his family to the town of Parramatta and left her in charge of his farm. She later returned to Sydney and became a nurse to some of the notable families of Sydney. Some time later, and by now respectable, she moved to a cottage on a small farm on Richmond Hill above the Hawkesbury.

In an account of her life written by Richard Cobald, the son of the employer from whom she stole the horse, her career was amalgamated for the purposes of romantic embellishment with that of Mary Haydock, afterwards Mary Reibey, the wife of Thomas Reibey and a leading figure in Sydney. Mary Haydock had been transported for stealing a pony. The Reibey family objected strongly to Cobald's licence, but the mistake was never rectified to their satisfaction. Mary Reibey became a leading business woman in Sydney, taking over a bakery and a general store with a wine and spirit licence and, after the death of her husband, a shipping business. She had seven large farms on the Hawkesbury River and three houses.

The King Of Iceland

Danish born George Jorgenson was one of' Australia's most colourful convicts. He visited Australia early in the 1 9th century as mate aboard the Lady Nelson which was engaged in doing survey work of the Australian coast under Lieutenant Grant. In 1804 he went sealing to New Zealand and then whaling off the Tasmanian coast. He claimed to have struck the first whale killed in the Derwent.

He took two Maoris and two Tahitians back to England and handed them over to Sir Joseph Banks, but three of them died. Jorgenson returned to Copenhagen, his birthplace, to command a small privateer in the naval war between Denmark and Britain. He was captured and became a prisoner of war in England. Sir Joseph Banks sent him to Iceland with a cargo of provisions for inhabitants who had been reduced to starvation point by the British blockade.

The Danish Governor had forbidden trade with the English, so the owner of the vessel deposed the Governor and established Jorgenson in his place. Jorgenson ruled for three weeks and introduced many popular reforms before an English vessel came and re-instated the Governor.

Jorgenson was taken back to England to be tried for breaking his parole and was imprisoned for a year. He was subsequently employed by the British Foreign Office as a secret service agent in Europe, but heavy gambling in London led him to steal. He was sentenced to transportation to Tasmania, and reached Hobart in 1826. He later became district constable at Oatlands and was one of the few who took an interest in the Aborignes and collected a vocabulary of their language. He was given 100 acres of land, but sold it and eventually died in poverty and obscurity.

A Snake Pit

Sir Henry Brown Hayes, a wealthy Irish convict who decided to stay on in Sydney after his release, made his home in the district he called Vaucluse because it reminded him of a beautiful valley in France. Sir Henry built a mansion, Vaucluse House, which afterwards was purchased and improved by the Australian statesman, William Charles Wentworth. Sir Henry soon discovered that the district was overrun with snakes, which were presumptuous enough to invade his house and even his bedroom. His remedy was to import 500 barrels of soil from Ireland with which he filled a trench around his house three feet wide and two feet deep. Oddly, he was never troubled by snakes again.

Sir Henry's transportation was caused by his abduction of an Irish heiress, Mary Pike. Before his crime he had been captain of the South Cork Militia and a Sheriff of County Cork. His desperate love for Miss Pike caused him to keep her a prisoner for eight hours hoping that he would soften her heart. When he produced a minister and a wedding ring she flung the ring at him and subsequently had a warrant issued for his arrest.

A convict chain gang.

Barclay's Tigers

Barclay's tigers were convicts under Lieutenant Barclay, who was in charge of those assigned to coal mining duties from the Port Arthur penal settlement, in the 1830s. The brutal Barclay was a systematic flogger and his charges became known by the symmetrical flogging striped on their backs.

Tolpuddle Martyrs

A group of activists who created a furore in England and were the forerunners there of trade unionism were sentenced to transportation to Australia. The group became known as the

Tolpuddle Martyrs. In 1833 they had attempted to found the first agricultural trade union in Dorset, demanding an increase in wages for agricultural workers from 7 shillings to 10 shillings a week. In Australia they were kept apart from one another and from other prisoners and worked in various occupations, from assignment to farmers to building construction. For the three years they were away from England, the continuation of their protest had borne fruit. Demonstrations and the resolutions of half a million people had led to reforms and some recognition of the rights of workers.

The Wild White Man

William Buckley, a six foot six former soldier, was among the convicts assigned to Lieutenant David Collins when a party landed at Sorrento in 1803 in an attempt to establish a settlement at Port Phillip. Collins chose Buckley for his manservant, but he used his greater freedom to slip away from the camp with three others and take refuge with the Aborigines. Before Collins abandoned the settlement 21 convicts had escaped to the bush but two-thirds of them were captured or had returned.

Among those who did not return were Buckley and two of his companions. Nearly 32 years later, on 12 July 1835, a party which John Batman had left in occupation at Indented Head was visited by the natives. One among them was of great stature, European in features and with the tatoo mark W. B. on one arm. After questioning, he was persuaded to say "bread" when a piece was offered to him. Within a few days he remembered other English words.

In later years a story purporting to have come from his own mouth of his adventures during the missing 32 years was published. He said that on leaving Collins' camp he made his way north along the bay shore and stayed near the sea in the hope that he might be picked up by a sealer or stray merchant vessel. He worked around the head of the bay and down the western shores into the Geelong district and then into the Otway Ranges.

For over 30 years he lived with the Geelong Aborigines, ranging northwards as far as the Yarra River but usually camping near the Youyng Ranges. He received a formal pardon and was for a time employed by the Port Phillip Association to liaise with the Aborigines. He was made a constable and interpreter to the Aborigines. He eventually moved to Tasmania where the Government gave him small posts like assistant storekeeper or gatekeeper until he retired on a pension in 1852.

The Man They Couldn't Hang

On 26 September 1803, Joseph Samuels was escorted from Sydney Gaol to a place of execution. He had been charged with having stolen money, a writing desk and other items belonging to one Mary Bryant. The authorities suspected that Samuels and an accomplice had murdered a constable while he was enquiring into the robbery, but they did not have sufficient evidence for a conviction. Before leaving the prisoners, the Reverend Samuel Marsden asked Samuels to unburden his conscience. Samuels declared that his accomplice had been accosted by the constable and had knocked him down and killed him.

At 10 a.m. Samuels and another prisoner mounted the execution cart The other prisoner, James Hardwick, was granted a reprieve at that point Samuels said a last prayer and the cart was driven from under him. The sudden tension on the rope caused it to snap and Samuels fell to the ground. Again the cart was brought under the gibbet and Joseph Samuels had a fresh noose placed about his neck. He was again launched, but the rope unravelled until Samuels legs trailed along the ground and the body was only half suspended. By this time Samuels was unconscious.

A third time the executioner prepared him for death, a fresh rope was placed around his neck and those who had been supporting him let him fall. However the rope also snapped and he fell to the ground. The Provost Marshall rushed off to see Governor King who granted a reprieve. Samuels was not reformed by his miraculous escape from death. He and some other convict escapees took a boat from Newcastle, New South Wales, and were not heard of again.

Lost in Tasmania

The first known white man to live with Aborigines was Samuel Jervis who claimed to be the son of Squire Jervis of Shenstone Park, Lichfield, England. When his father died he was left in the care of his uncle, Captain John Jervis. who took him to sea. In 1789 Jervis's ship the Regent Fox put into the Tasmanian shore near what is now the Tamar River and a boat crew landed to look for water. Samuel Jervis hid in the bush as he was afraid his uncle intended to maroon him on an island so that he could claim title to the Shenstone Park Estate. He was captured by natives and became one of their tribe in the Quamby region of Tasmania. Twenty-five years later in the Hadspen district he saw a white man for the first time since leaving ship. He left his tribe to live with a family of settlers named Cox and assumed their surname. He died in June 1891 at Launceston.

The Tasmanian Highlands in winter

True Patriots All

The first theatrical performance in Australia took place on 1 6 January 1796 when a cast of convicts performed Edward Young's play The Revenge The play was preceded by a now famous prologue which was spoken by George Barrington, actor and convict, who was known as the Prince of Pickpockets. A famous couplet from the prologue which has been often repeated down the years was:

True patriots all: for be it understood
We left our country for our country's good.

A Useful Tree

Cabbage tree hats were popular headwear in pioneering times and they were just one of the many useful benefits derived from this forest tree of New South Wales. The hearts of the cabbage tree palm were as tasty as cabbage itself, while the big outside leaves were used to make a long-lasting and waterproof thatching. Cabbage tree hats were made from the leaves which were bleached, split into ribbons and plaited while damp. The straw coloured hats were long lasting and could be scrubbed and washed. They were light and cool and ideal for the hot Australian climate.

The Convicts' Lament

Convicts were sentenced to Transportation (which many initially viewed as worse than death) for the most trivial of crimes. Seven years in a penal colony for stealing a sixpenny book was a common sentence. Shackled in irons on the convict ships, flogged by overseers for the slightest offence, only the strongest survived to become hardy pioneers of an alien land.

In 1840 reports of the brutality inflicted on prisoners, the efforts of reformers and the protests of the colonial population itself caused the British parliament to discontinue Transportation to New South Wales.

It was too late to save young Valentine Marshall, sentenced to Transportation to Van Diemen's Land for merely watching a house at Nottingham go up in flames:

Good people give attention and listen to my tale,
The truth of my misfortunes I quickly will reveal.
I being young and foolish, my years just turned sixteen
When Judge Littledale did me transport for being on Colwick Green
But now I'm in Van Dieman's Land, where happy I could be,
Were it not for my parents, their grief I can't relieve.
But I hope the Lord is goodness, will blessing to them send
And such troubles in Old England I hope they soon may end.

From a verse sent to his friends, 1834

Botany Bay

The best known ballad handed down from the days of transportation has a lively spirit which no doubt belied the mood of most convicts as they set out from England for a life of hardship and servitude at Botany Bay:

Farewell to old England for ever,
Farewell to my rum calls as well;
Farewell to the well-known old Bailey,
Where I used for to cut such a swell.

Chorus
Singing toorali-oorali-ad-dity
Singing toorali-oorali-ay
Singing toorali-oorali-ad-dity

Well, we-re bound for Botany Bay.
There's the captain as is our commander,
There's the bo'sun and all the ship's crew,
There's the first and second class passengers,
Now's what we poor convicts goes through.

'Taint leavin' old England we cares about
'Taint cos we mispels wot we knows,
But becos all are light-fingered sentry
Hops around with a log on our toes.

Oh, had I the wings of a turtle dove!
I'd soar on my pinions so high,
Slap bang to the arms of my Dolly love,
And in her sweet presence I'd die.

Now all you young Dookies and Duchesses,
Take warning from what I've to say,
Mind all is your own as you touchesses,
Or you'll find us in Botany Bay.

Poetic Broadside

The first Presbyterian Minister in Australia, John Dunmore Lang, became a politician and indefatigable pamphleteer and a doughty critic of the Colonial establishment. At one stage he got heartily sick of the naming of places after Colonial dignitaries or political figures in England and he penned this scathing poem in 1824:

'Twas said of Greece two thousand years ago,
That every stone i' the land had got a name.
Of New South Wales too, men will soon say so;
But every stone there seems to get the same.
"Macquarie" for a name is all the go:
The old Scotch Governor was fond of fame,
Macquarie Street, Place, Port, Fort Town, Lake, River:
"Lachlan Macquarie, Esquire, Governor" for ever!

I like the native names, as Parramatta,
And Illawarra, and Woolloomooloo;
Nandowra, Woogarora, Bulkamatta,
Tomah, Toongabbie, Mittagong, Meroo;
Buckobble, Cumleroy, and Coolangatta,
The Warragumby, Bargo, Burradoo;
Cookbundoon, Carrabaiga, Wingecarribee,
The Wollondilly, Yurumbon, Bungarribee.

I hate your Goulburn Downs and Goulburn Plains,
And Goulburn River and the Goulburn Range,
A Mount Goulburn and Goulburn Vale! One's brains

Are turned with Goulburns! Vile scorbutic mange
For immortaility! Had I the reins
()f government a fortnight, I would change
These Downing Street appellatives, and give
The country names that should deserve to live.

Yes! let some badge of liberty appear
On every mountain and on every plain
Where Britain's power is known, or far or near,
That freedom there may have an endless reign!
Then though she die, in some revolving year,
A race may rise to make her live again!
The future slave may lisp the patriot's name
And his breast kindle with a kindred flame!

Dungaree Settlers

By 1795 the colony boasted a modest and very egalitarian community of farmers, mostly ex- convicts, who brought fresh produce to Sydney Town from small holdings in the "Currajong Mountains"; from Windsor and Richmond on the Hawkesbury River; and various points along the Parramatta River. The life of these settlers was simple and hard but no doubt not quite so difficult as it was for those still in bondage. They took up their grants with generally no experience, no animals and very little assistance from the government. Added to these privations were skirmishes with the blacks and seven disastrous floods in fifteen years. Nevertheless this remarkably tenacious and industrious group survived and eventually grew to become the providors for the colony. They were easily distinguished on their journeys to Sydney on market days by their distinctive blue dress made from imported blue Dungaree Indian cotton.

By 1830, accounts of the settlers listed numerous crops including corn and wheat peaches, figs, gooseberries, currants, lemons, oranges, melons, peas, beans, pumpkins and potatoes.

Along the Hawkesbury the community also produced daughters, a rare treasure in a penal settlement where men far outnumbered women, and probably for safety as much as for practicality, in a community where women also laboured in the fields, the females sometimes dressed as men.

Overlanders rounding up a straggler

A cartoon showing the deposed Governor Bligh arrested from beneath his bed

The Rum Rebellion

On the 26 January 1808 the New South Wales Corps, with drums beating and the band playing "The British Grenadiers", marched on Government House and placed the Governor, William Bligh of Bounty fame, under house arrest

The Rum Rebellion was so named because of the participation of the New South Wales Corps in the rum trade. Bligh earned the antipathy of the Corps when, on his arrival in the colony in 1806, he had immediately ordered a stop to the importation of stills and the illegal trafficking of liquor over which the officers and the elite settlers held a lucrative monopoly.

Bligh was kept under house arrest for one year and then agreed to sail for England in the 'Porpoise'. Instead he took command of the ship and put in to Hobart before returning to England where he was exonerated of the charges brought against him by the Corps.

The rum trade continued to be one of the constant problems of colonial Governors. In 1844 Governor Gipps wrote:

"Drunkeness, it is well known has ever long been the prevailing vice of New South Wales and the fruitful source of more than half the crimes committed in it"

Jim Jones

Even if the transportees survived the rigors of the voyage to the colony, their troubles were only just beginning as the following folksong tells us

Oh, listen for a moment, lads,
And hear me tell my tale;
How, o'er the sea from England's shore,
I was compelled to sail.
The jury says, "He's guilty, sir!"
And the judge says he— "For life,
Jim Jones, I'm sending you
Across the stormy sea.

"And take my tip, before you ship
To join the iron gang,
Don't be too gay at Botany Bay,
Or else you'll surely hang," says he,
"And after that, Jim Jones,
High upon the gallows tree
The crows will pick your bones.

"You'll have no chance for mischief then
Remember what I say:
They'll flog the mischief out of you
When you get to Botany Bay!"
The waves were high upon the sea,
The winds blew up in gales;
I'd rather be drowned in misery
Than go to New South Wales.

For night and day the irons clang,
And, like poor galley slaves,
We toil and moil and when we die
Must fill dishonoured graves.
But by and by I'll break my chains;
Into the bush I'll go;
And join the brave bushrangers there —
Jack Donahoe and Co

And some dark night when everything
Is silent in the town
I'll shoot the tyrants one and all
And shoot the floggers down.
I'll give the law a little shock —
Remember what I say,
They'll yet regret they sent Jim Jones
In chains to Botany Bay.

The Transport Ships

In June 1870 three convict transport ships arrived in Port Jackson, they were the Neptune, Scarborough and Surprise. The conditions on the transports were notorious but the toll of death and sickness amongst transportees on these ships caused the Reverend Richard Johnson, the first Anglican Chaplain in New South Wales, to write the following letter:

"There were on:

The Neptune—520 convicts, but 163 died on board and 269 landed sick.

The Scarborough—252 convicts, but 68 died on board and 96 landed sick. The Surprise—211 convicts, but 42 died on board and 121 landed sick.

This short calculation given me will support what I am going to relate.

I have been on board these different ships—was first on board the Surprise— went down amongst the convicts, where I beheld a sight truly shocking to the feelings of humanity, a great number of them lying, some half and others nearly quite naked, without either bed or bedding, unable to turn to help themselves. Spoke to them as I passed along but the smell was so offensive, I could scarcely bear it

I then went on board the Scarborough, proposed to go down among them but was dissuaded from it by the Captain. The Neptune was still more wretched and intolerable, therefore I never attempted it.

Some of these unhappy people died after the ships came into the harbour, before they could be taken on shore; and were seen lying naked on the rocks took an occasion to represent this to his Excellency, in consequence of which immediate orders were sent on board, that those who died on board should be carried to the opposite North Shore to be buried.

The landing of these people was truly affecting and shocking, great numbers were not able to walk, nor move hand or foot. Such were slung over the ship's side in the same manner as they would sling a cask or box, or anything of that nature. Upon their being brought up to the open air, some fainted, some died upon deck, and others in the boat before they reached the shore.

When come on shore many were not able to walk, to stand or to stir themselves in the least. Hence some were led by others, while some crept upon their hands and knees, and some were carried on the backs of others.

The complaints they had to make were not less affecting to the ear than their outward condition was to the eye. The usage they met with on board, according to their own story, was truly shocking. Sometimes for days, nay, for a considerable time together, they had been to the middle in water, chained together, hand and leg—even the sick not exempted—nay many died with the chains upon them. Promises, entreaties, were all in vain, and it was not till a few days before they made the harbour, that they were released out of irons.

The greatest complaints by far were from those persons who had come in the Neptune. No wonder that they should be so afflicted—no wonder to hear them groaning, and crying, and making the most bitter lamentations."

Bushrangers

A History Of Bushranging

The bushranger Martin Cash in old age.

Fact and legend have become so mixed in stories of Australian bushrangers, and the facts are so little in need of embellishment for the telling of a good story, that a short and selective history of bushranging in Australia will set the scene for the more apocryphal tales that exist in Australian folklore.

The systematic practice of highway robbery, usually by single bushrangers or small gangs, flourished during two periods and was revived for a third short period by the Kelly gang. The first epoch of bushranging was concerned with convict escapees, the second era was the result of the lawless adventures of freemen tempted by rich convoys of gold.

The term bushranger first came to be used for the convict escapees. In Tasmania the escapees were at first called "bolters". Convicts who escaped from a signed service or road gangs took to the bush to avoid recapture. Not finding much to live on they were compelled to resort to robbery for their sustenance. Tasmania, being the gaol for the most hardened criminals, produced the earliest and most violent bushrangers. Governor Bligh expressed concern in 1807 about the bushrangers who were annoying Governor Collins in Tasmania and in 1809 he reported that some of the crew of the Porpoise had joined a body of 60 bushrangers who were infesting the road in inland New South Wales.

Collins and later Governor Davey tried amnesty as a means of clearing the bush of wandering gangs, but the measures proved ineffective. Among bushrangers mentioned in amnesty

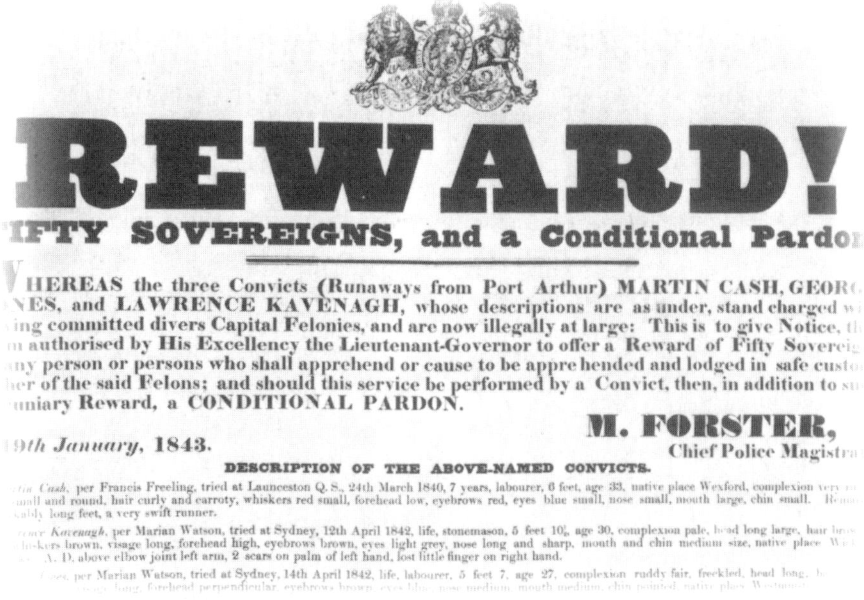

REWARD!

IFTY SOVEREIGNS, and a Conditional Pardo

HEREAS the three Convicts (Runaways from Port Arthur) MARTIN CASH, GEOR NES, and LAWRENCE KAVENAGH, whose descriptions are as under, stand charged w ing committed divers Capital Felonies, and are now illegally at large: This is to give Notice, t n authorised by His Excellency the Lieutenant-Governor to offer a Reward of Fifty Soverei ny person or persons who shall apprehend or cause to be apprehended and lodged in safe custo her of the said Felons; and should this service be performed by a Convict, then, in addition to su uniary Reward, a CONDITIONAL PARDON.

M. FORSTER,
Chief Police Magistra

***9th January*, 1843.**

DESCRIPTION OF THE ABOVE-NAMED CONVICTS.

tin Cash, per Francis Freeling, tried at Launceston Q. S., 24th March 1840, 7 years, labourer, 6 feet, age 33, native place Wexford, complexion very small and round, hair curly and carroty, whiskers red small, forehead low, eyebrows red, eyes blue small, nose small, mouth large, chin small. Rem ably long feet, a very swift runner.

rence Kavenagh, per Marian Watson, tried at Sydney, 12th April 1842, life, stonemason, 5 feet 10½, age 30, complexion pale, head long large, hair br hiskers brown, visage long, forehead high, eyebrows brown, eyes light grey, nose long and sharp, mouth and chin medium size, native place W A. D. above elbow joint left arm, 2 scars on palm of left hand, lost little finger on right hand.

ones, per Marian Watson, tried at Sydney, 14th April 1842, life, labourer, 5 feet 7, age 27, complexion ruddy fair, freckled, head long,

A reward notice for Martin Cash and his companions a notorious group of escaped convicts and bushrangers. Cash escaped from Port Arthur by swimming offshore from Eaglehawk Neck Cash once captured 23 men, tied them up and ransacked a house they were in. He was re-captured, eventually released for good behaviour and became caretaker of the gardens at Government House.

offers were Michael Howe and John Whitehead. Both took advantage of the offer but were back in the bush within six months and had joined up to lead a notorious gang.

The establishment in December 1821 of a penal settlement at Macquarie harbour on the west coast, where discipline was extremely severe and escape very difficult, resulted in a revival of bushranging. Some prisoners escaped by land and they suffered great hardships and privation. The most notorious of them was Pierce the Cannibal who escaped in 1822 with eight others. Only Pierce survived death or recapture and he murdered and ate his companions one by one. After he was left alone he lived for a long time by plundering lonely settlements, but he was eventually recaptured and returned to Macquarie harbour.

The principal gang in Tasmania was that of Matthew Brady, who with 12 companions stole a boat at Macquarie harbour in 1824 and landed nine days later near the mouth of the Derwent. For nearly two years the gang raided settlements from Launceston to Sorell. Brady forbade unnecessary violence and boasted that he had never killed a man intentionally. He severely punished members of the gang who were brutal to women. In 1826 his gang was betrayed and broken up and he was captured by John Batman. The island thereafter had comparative peace, although a small gang infested the northern settlements in 1832 and 1833 and in the early '40s Martin Cash, with two companions, committed many robberies in central Tasmania.

Serious bushranging on the mainland did not commence until 1833 when 34 bushrangers were hanged. In 1824 the raids of escapees caused the proclamation of martial law west of Mount York from August to December. In 1826 a gang of seven had a fight with police near Bathurst and between 1827-30 Donahoe and Underwood harried the Hawkesbury/Nepean settlers.

"Mad" Dan Morgan, who operated in the Riverina and Northern Victoria, is considered to have been the most brutal of the non-convict bushrangers. He is seen shooting a pursuer in an affray at Copabella.

This was the "Bold Jack Donahoe" of the old bush song, although Donahoe was killed by a settler and not by police as the song suggests. Underwood is said to have been killed by his mates when they discovered he was keeping a diary—a prelude to turning King's evidence.

By 1830 bushranging had become so prevalent that the Legislative Council passed a Bushranging Act. Among other things it provided that all suspected persons might be apprehended without a warrant, that anyone carrying arms might be arrested, that anyone suspected of having arms might be searched, that police might enter or break into any house by day or by night seize firearms found there in and arrest the inmates, and when convicted, robbers and house breakers were to be condemned to death and executed on the third day thereafter.

The Act was followed soon after by an outbreak near Bathurst. Nearly 80 convicts escaped and joined into a gang but after a week or two it had dwindled to 18 well armed and desperate men who beat off a body of settlers and two detachments of mounted police before they were captured by a company of the 39th Regiment. The hanging provisions of the Act were vigorously enforced and for some years bushranging died down, but it revived again in 1839-42 with the lead given by John Lynch, who is believed to have committed at least nine murders before he was hanged in 1842, at the age of 29.

William Westwood (JackeyJackey), who had been transported in 1837 when only 16 years old, escaped in the Goulburn district in 1840 and for some time robbed mail coaches on the Bungendore road. Growing more daring, he frequented the main southern road and even visited Sydney, but in 1841 he was captured and sentenced to penal servitude for life. He escaped from Cockatoo Island and was sent to Port Arthur where he escaped again, but was caught in Hobart and sent to Norfolk Island. There in 1846 he headed a riot, killed four policemen and was hanged at the age of 26.

"Stuck Up — an encounter between bushrangers and a coach on a New South Wales road. From the Sydney Illustrated News supplement of May, 1870.

There were a number of less celebrated bushrangers who took to the road in the late '30s and who operated from northern New South Wales to the Dandenong Ranges near Melbourne and in settlements east of Gawler in South Australia, but by the '40s settlement along the main roads and the availability of police protection made the rewards for bushranging entirely disproportionate to the risks.

With the coming of gold the face of' the eastern districts of rural Australia changed from sparsely settled farming districts. The country in both forest and cleared areas became scattered with mines. Roads were cut through dense bush to get to gold bearing regions and small farmers established themselves in remote gullies and bush areas to struggle for an existence. It was often the sons of these small farmers who took up the bushranging trade. The "wild colonial boys", who saw miners making fortunes by luck rather than hard work, wanted their share of the lightly won wealth.

The free born bushranger of the '50s and '60s had lots of allies. The whole countryside was often in league with them and protected them against their natural enemies, the police. They stole gold from the townsfolk and horses from the squatters, but that did not injure the small farmer class from which they sprang.

The career of Frank Gardner exemplifies this. Many times he was either captured or surrounded by the police, but either his guards could be bribed or some inept foolishness by officialdom allowed him to go free.

The great gang of the bushranging '60s was led by Ben Hall. It raided Bathurst then the second town of the Colony; it stuck up many gold escorts and fought long fights with the police; it besieged a magistrate in his own homestead and held him to ransom so that his wife, Mrs. Keightley, had to ride to save her husband's life.

At Bangbang three of Hall's gang and a couple of police constables exchanged 40 shots without doing any serious damage. At Canowindra three bushrangers, Ben Hall, John Gilbert

Ben Hall.

and John O'Malley, held up the entire township for three days issuing passes for those who wished to go out of town on urgent errands. of their visit to Candowindra was to take a holiday from the bush and they stayed at the hotel where they ordered entertainment and enjoyed the company of the townsfolk. Their haunt was the Weddin Mountain, where they easily eluded police parties in the tangled gullies and baffling scrub. The Ben Hall gang never numbered more than six and Hall was only 25 when he took the lead. The others ranged from that age down to 17.

By 1846 two of Hall's gang had been shot during attacks on stations and one had surrendered himself on the advice of a Catholic priest. The three remaining, Hall, Gilbert and Dunn, decided on a major exploit. They stationed themselves on a hill near Jugiong and soon collected about 60 prisoners. Everyone who came by was struck up, robbed and forced to sit in the bush out of sight of the road. Presently a mounted policeman came along and was ordered to surrender. When he refused they exchanged shots and he gave up and took his place with the 60.

At last came the great prize, the overland mail coach, with a constable as guard and a sergeant and sub-inspector as escort. Shots were exchanged, the sergeant was killed, the sub-inspector surrendered, the mail guard ran away and a police magistrate who was a passenger helped to throw the mail bags out of the coach. The 60 captives, guarded by one man, remained passive. When it was over Gilbert walked over to his victim's body and said, "He was a brave fellow, I don't like to shoot a man and he's the first man I ever shot."

In fact the Hall gang did not have a reputation for violence and often avoided a fight.

A group of policemen who took part in the siege of the Glenrowon Inn

People who defied them boldly were often allowed to go unharmed and there is a story of William Macleay who came across the gang and a group they had held up. Macleay ordered his boy to drive on slowly while he walked by the horse with a loaded rifle in his hand. The gang at once rode off into the bush and did not disturb him until he got into his buggy again. They then fired a couple of shots. but disappeared when he returned their fire. Macleay actually stopped to talk to the prisoners, but found them too cowed even to answer him, much less to make any escape attempt.

While the bushrangers' trade was profitable and they were able to avoid the police almost with ease and good humour on both sides, the mood changed when, early in 1865, one of the gang shot a constable at Collector and wounded several others in skirmishes which followed.

The bush came alive with police and both Gilbert and Hall were shot to death, the latter receiving volley after volley from his pursuers. Fifteen bullets were found in his body. In two and a half years the whole gang had committed ten mail robberies, stolen 23 race horses, raided 21 stores and private houses and killed two men.

A bushranger of a very different type, Daniel Morgan, known as "Mad Dan", was active in the southern districts of New South Wales. He rivalled the worst of the convict bushrangers in brutality, although there is a suggestion that he was a schizophrenic personality as he often displayed kindliness and courtesy to his prisoners. At his worst he shot down unarmed and sleeping men and tortured women. In 1865, in response to a challenge from the Victorian police, he crossed the Murray and held up traffic and station owners between Wangaratta and Benalla. On 8 April he visited Peechalba Station some 15 miles northwest of Wangaratta, bailed up the entire household for the night and was shot next morning by a station hand.

The notorious bushrangers, Tom and John Clarke, photographed at Braidwood gaol.

Another notorious gang was that of the Clarke brothers who operated between Goulburn and Monaro from 1865 -67. They had an amazing family history. The father

A depiction of the escape of the bushranger Thomas Clarke from Braidwood Gaol in 1865. In the next eight months he stole three racehorses, robbed a post office, three stores and many travellers, stuck up a mail coach and killed a policeman.

died in gaol; of four uncles, one was shot by police in a raid, two were convicted of highway robbery and the fourth was accessory to the murder of a policeman. The family lived by cattle duffing and horse stealing until the police tried to arrest them and then they took to bushranging. The second brother, James, was convicted of receiving stolen property from the Ben Hall gang. Thomas, the eldest, escaped from Braidwood Gaol where he had been committed on a charge of robbery in October 1865 and in the next eight months stole three race horses, robbed a post office, three stores and many travellers on the roads between Braidwood and Moruya, stuck up the Araluen mail and killed a policeman. His youngest brother, John, joined him in the bush and in 11 months they held up six mail coaches, robbed innumerable travellers and killed four special constables. Patrick Connell, an uncle, frequently accompanied Thomas, and William Scott and James Griffin were also members of the gang. After the murder of the constables a reward of £500 was offered for their capture and they promptly celebrated the distinction by sticking up four mail coaches in a fortnight. However on 27 April 1867 they were surrounded at night in a settler's hut by 15 troopers and the next day they surrendered without a struggle. They were tried in Sydney and hanged.

A portrait of Ned Kelly the day before his execution.

Isolated cases of bushranging continued to occur after the execution of the Clarkes. The best known of the later criminals was Frederick Ward, known as Captain Thunderbolt, an ex-convict born at Windsor, who from December 1864 to May 1870 lived at large in the area from Newcastle north to Manilla. He robbed many mail coaches

Scene of the attack on the inn at Glenrowen.

and held up many travellers before he was shot on 25 May. He is usually reckoned to be the last of the New South Wales bushrangers.

The other Colonies were less troubled. In Queensland there was only one professional bushranger, Alpin MacPherson, better known as the Wild Scotsman. In Victoria, the most notable of a small number of bushrangers was Harry Power, who was gaoled for horse stealing in 1855, escaped in 1869 and took to the bush in the Beechworth district, robbing freely until he was captured again in 1870. The government then set a price of £500 upon each of them, alive or dead, and the bandits entered a career of reckless crime in the regions of Benalla, Euroa, Mansfield and Beechworth. They had numerous connections and sympathisers in the district and, as they never molested a woman or victimised a poor man, they had a certain popularity.

From 1870 onwards Australia was largely free from bushrangers for about eight years. Then came the astounding feats of the Kelly gang. Ned Kelly, the leader of the gang, had consorted with Power, who thus became a link between the bushrangers of the '60s and the final eruption of the late '70s. The Kelly gang has its beginnings in the lawlessness of Kelly's father and the family of his mother. Ned Kelly's father, John Kelly, was transported from Tipperary in Ireland to Tasmania and after serving his term became a cattle stealer in the Wallan district. He married the daughter of James Quinn another cattle stealer, and they had three sons, Ned, Jim and Dan, and four daughters. The Quinns and the Kellys moved to 11 Mile Creek near Greta, a few miles from Glenrowan, in the area which came to be known as "Kelly country". Here they carried on their old trade in stolen cattle and horses and incurred a series of arrests and short terms if imprisonment. Then Ned shot a constable in the arm when he tried to arrest Dan and, after Mrs. Kelly and two neighbours were arrested for subsequently attacking the constable, Ned Kelly, at the age of 24, formed his famous gang. It included Dan, aged 17, Steve Hart of Wangaratta, aged 18, and Joe Byrne, born near Beechworth, aged 21. They hid in the hills as a reward was offered for their apprehension. When a party of policeman came upon them in the Wombat Hills they shot three of them.

Two of their most celebrated exploits were robberies at Euroa and Jerilderie. At Euroa the

After the siege of Glenrowan the capture of Ned kelly and the death of his fellows in the Glenrowan Inn, Joe Byrne's Body was strung up outside the Benalla police station and photoqraphed.

gang determined to rob the National Bank, which stood only 50 yards from the station on the main north-eastern railway. Three miles distant was Younghusband's estate and the gang decided to rest and refresh themselves there before making their raid on the bank. They bailed up Younghusband's station, shut up all the hands in the store and imprisoned a party who were driving past.

Ned Kelly's armour fashioned from ploughshares.

The telegraph lines were cut to prevent communication and the gang then ate and slept in watches. After compelling one of their prisoners to write a small cheque on the bank they left Byrne to watch the store and proceeded to Euroa. The bank was already closed but Ned begged the clerk to let them in and cash the cheque. Dan and Steve Hart went to the back. When the clerk admitted him, Ned presented his revolver and at the same time the others forced the bank entrance. They forced Scott, the manager, to hand over the keys and took over £2,000. Kelly then commandeered the manager's wagonette and took all the people from the bank back with him to Younghusband's and shut them in. He warned them to remain there for three hours or he would meet them again and shoot them.

The Jerilderie raid took place two months later on 9 February 1879. Jerilderie is in New South Wales, about 60 miles across the Murray River, and the Kellys' perpetrated this raid partly from bravado, because the police of New South Wales had derided those of Victoria for their inability to arrest the gang. They entered the township at midnight and went to the police station, where Ned called out that a murder had been committed at a local hotel. As soon as the police came out unarmed, the gang seized them and locked them up in their own prison. Then they dressed themselves in the troppers' clothes and got the police farrier to shoe their horses. Next they took possession of the Royal Hotel, used it for holding their prisoners, and then robbed the Bank of New South Wales of £2,140. Ned made a speech to the people in the hotel as Dan Kelly and Hart rode theatrically down the street flourishing their revolvers and singing.

Ned Kelly at bay.

Rewards from two Governments now totalled over £8,000 and for 16 months the gang remained quiet, but an accomplice named Aaron Sherritt, on the promise of £4,000, agreed to lead the police under the direction of Superintendent Hare to their hiding place. On 27 June 1880 Sherritt hid a police party in his cottage but Dan Kelly and Byrne caused a policeman to be enticed to the door and shot him. The gang then hastended to Glenrowan and took possession of the little township. They tore up the rails of the railway line at a point where it crossed a ravine. All strangers who came along were interned in the hotel.

Meanwhile the authorities in Melbourne had sent off a special train with police and black trackers, but a school master named Thomas Curnon escaped from the Kellys' custody and stopped the train a little way from Glenrowan. This was at dusk and police immediately laid seige to the hotel and telegraphed to Melbourne for a small canon. During the evening several of the captives were released from the hotel and in the morning the rest of the captives were set free.

Suddenly the police were fired on from behind. Ned Kelly had got through the police cordon in the dark and, clad in rough head and body armour, was firing at the police from the rear. He was shot in the legs and captured. In the afternoon the building was set on fire and the bodies of the other three members of the gang were found in the ruins.

Ned Kelly was taken to Melbourne and convicted of the murder of the Mansfield police and hanged on 11 November 1880.

The macabre nature of the last moments of the Kelly gang, with Kelly, clad in armour made from ploughshares, calmly walking among his enemies and firing on them, his comrades firing on the 50 police who were sending a withering fire on the little weatherboard hotel, a crowd of spectators watching from the distance and the final conflagration, make the most memorable scene in bushranging history.

The Kelly gang locked the Jerilderie police up in their own gaol and then robbed the town's bank.

A Prophecy

Three weeks and four days after he condemned the bushranger, Ned Kelly, to death Sir Redmond Barry took ill, went to bed and died. His death occurred only a few days after Kelly had been executed in the Melbourne gaol. Sir Redmond was said to have been affected by Kelly's last words to him. After passing the sentence of death he concluded with the words, "and may the Lord have mercy on your soul". Kelly replied, "Yes, I will meet you there in a bigger court than this."

Black Jack's Last Words

Two Aborigines, Black Jack and Mosquito, led raids on the settlers in Tasmania during the "Black War" at the time of Governor Arthur. According to James Bonwick in his book The Last of the Tasmanians, published in London in 1870, Black Jack and Mosquito were sentenced to be hanged. On the day of their execution, 25 February 1825, they were exhorted to pray by the Chaplain, the Rev. W. Bedford. Mosquito maintained a solid silence, but Black Jack exclaimed, "You pray yourself I too bloody frightened to pray."

Chinese Bushranger

Sam Poo, the Chinese bushranger, was active between Mudgee and Coonabarabran, New South Wales, in 1865. Challenged by Casba Ward, the Chinese bushranger called out, "You policeman, me shootee you!" and wounded the trooper. Sam Poo was hunted down and captured, convicted of attempted murder and hanged.

Chinese arriving on the goldfields.

Michael Howe, second Lieutenant Governor of Tasmania.

Governor Of The Rangers

Michael Howe (1787-1818) was one of the most notorious of the bushrangers of early Van Diemen's Land. A former sailor, he found the discipline harsh, and deserted to become a highwayman in England. He was caught and sent to Van Diemen's Land. but escaped soon after his arrival to begin a life as a bushranger.

The amiable Governor Davey tried to ease the problems of the lawlessness by offering an amnesty to bushrangers if they surrendered themselves before a certain day. Every bushranger came in. Michael Howe among them, but after their holiday they all left together with a man named Whitehead as the leader of the band. Then began a period of burning, looting and bloody conflict with settlers which ended when they were ambushed by soldiers. Whitehead fell mortally wounded and his last request to Howe was to cut off his head to prevent anyone obtaining the promised reward for its capture.

Howe was now captain of the gang and was attended by an Aborigine called Black Mary. The headquarters were close to a marsh near Oatlands which is still known as Howe's Marsh. Howe was a strict disciplinarian, taking oaths of obedience upon the prayer book and employing the lash to correct irregularities. He often read aloud to his gang from the Bible.

Ambushed again, Howe was separated from his gang and pursued by the military with only Black Mary for company. As the soldiers gained on him he turned on her raised his musket, fired and severely wounded her before escaping to the mountains. After Black Mary recovered, she led parties of soldiers to Howe's haunts but they were unable to track him down. He then began a remarkable correspondence with Governor Davey addressing himself to the "Governor of the Town" and describing himself as the "Governor of the Rangers". He proposed a conditional surrender and the Governor sent a Captain Nairne to treat with the bushranger. Howe petitioned for a free pardon but Lieutenant Governor Davey offered a pardon only for crimes committed in the bush.

He continued his acts of terrorism and Lieutenant Governor Sorrel promised a full pardon pending Governor Macquarie's consent. Howe came to Hobart enjoying great popularity, but fled to the bush again after rumours that he was to be detained on a murder charge. Large rewards were offered for his capture or death and he was killed in 1818 by a solider named Warburton near the Shannon River. Legend has it that he was tracked and lured into the trap by Black Mary.

Dan Morgan shot and captured.

Ballads of the Bushrangers

Many different forces were at work to drive a man to bushranging and as the following song reveals some were feared and others were admired.

DUNN, GILBERT AND BEN HALL

Come all you wild colonials
And listen to my tale
A story of bush rangers' deeds
I will to you unveil.
'Tis of those gallant heroes,
Game fighters one and all;
And we'll sit and sing, long live the King.
Dunn, Gilbert and Ben Hall.

Frank Gardiner was a bushranger
Of terrible renown;
He robbed the Forbes gold escort,
And eloped with Kitty Brown.
But in the end they lagged him,
Two-and-thirty years in all.
"We must avenge the Darkie,"
Says Dunn, Gilbert and Ben Hall . . .

Ben Hall he was a squatter
Who owned six hundred head;
A peaceful man he was until
Arrested by Sir Fred.
His home burned down,
his wife cleared out,
His cattle perished all.
"They'll not take me a second time,"
Says valiant Ben Hall.

"Hand over all your watches
And the banknotes in your purses.
All travellers must pay toll to us
We don't care for your curses.
We are the rulers of the roads,
We've seen the troopers fall,
We want your gold and money,"
Says Dunn, Gilbert and Ben Hall.

"Next week we'll visit Goulburn
And clear the banks out there;
So if you see the peelers,
Just tell them to beware;
Some day to Sydney city
We mean to pay a call,
And we'll take the whole damn country!"
Say Dunn, Gilbert and Ben Hall.

Andrew Scott alias
'Captain Moonlite'.

JACK DONAHUE

A life that is free as the bandit's of old
When Rome was the prey of warriors bold
Who knew how to buy gallant soldiers with gold,
Is the life, full of danger,
Of Jack the bushranger,
Of brave Donahue!

If Ireland lies groaning, a hand at her throat,
Which foreigners have from the recreants bought,
Forget not the lessons our fathers have taught.
Though our Isle's full of danger,
And held by the stranger,
Be brave and be true!

I've left the old Island's hospitable shores,
The land of the Emmets, the Tones and the Moores;
But liberty o'er me her scalding tear pours,
And she points to the manger,
Where he was a stranger,
And perished for you.

Then hurl me to crime and brand me with shame,
But think not to baulk me, my spirit to tame,
For I'll fight to the last in old Ireland's name,
Though I be a bushranger,
You are still a stranger,
And I'm Donahue.

Golden Years

Hargraves finds gold — 12 February l 85 l .

The First Find

Edward Hammond Hargraves was the first man to discover gold in Australia and he received an award from the authorities in Sydney of £500. Hargraves had led an adventurous life before his gold strike. As a merchant seaman he had arrived at Sydney in 1832. After a few months on a station he joined a crew of a French fishing schooner to get beches-de-mer in the Torres Straits. All but seven of the crew died from Typhus at Batavia. Hargraves returned to Australia in 1834 and followed pastoral pursuits, traversing a good deal of the western foothill districts of New South Wales. He had a station on the Manning River and subsequently at Gosford but, disgusted with poor returns from cattle sales, he sailed for the Californian gold diggings and had a fair success there at the Woods Creek field.

In California he repeatedly assured friends that he knew of places in New South Wales of exactly the same kind where gold must be found sooner or later As soon as he had made enough money he went back to New South Wales, reaching Sydney on 7 January 1851. He immediately set out for the rough valleys beyond Bathurst, picking up a young bushman, John Listel on the way. On 12 Febuary they washed the first pan of gold-bearing gravel at the junction of the Summer Hill and Lewis Ponds Creeks. He confirmed this discovery by further samplings of creek gravel over an area of 70 by 40 miles in the Macquarie Valley and hastened back to Sydney to bargain with the authorities for £500 before he disclosed the localities of the gold-bearing creeks. The Government, however, insisted that he must trust their generosity so he named the localities and within three months,400 diggers were camped at the scene of the first discovery, while others were prospecting in the neighbouring valleys. Hargraves was appointed Commissioner of Crown Land and in October 1853 was granted a sum of £10,000 by the New South Wales Legislature.

A gold digger in NSW displays his find.

A Different Strike

The scene of the first important gold discovery in Victoria, Clunes, 20 miles north of Ballarat subsequently became the scene of bitter fights between miners and mine owners. The gold seekers of Clunes found that the bulk of ore was in quartz reefs requiring expensive shaft sinking. Companies were formed to exploit the reefs and many of the miners who worked were Cornish immigrants.

As the shafts went deeper the miners began to complain that safety measures were inadequate and the working day too long. In September 1873 miners at the Lothair mine went on strike. The management imported cheap Chinese labour from Adelaide and when they arrived a riot began. The miners converged on the Lothair mine and wrecked buildings and then set up a barricade of wagons and tree trunks at the junction of the Ballarat and Clunes roads. The Chinese, escorted by troopers, arrived in a convoy of coaches to be met by a shower of stones. The miners then stormed the coaches and set about them until orders were given for the coach drivers to take them back to Ballarat. The management subsequently agreed to the men's demand for a shorter Saturday shift and the Lothair mine resumed production.

When the alluvial gold of the eary mining days dwindled mining consortiums were formed to sink deep lead quartz mines. Quartz crushing plants then extracted the ore.

Historic Legacy

Australia was left a great historic legacy by the discoverer of one of the biggest finds of gold on the New South Wales' fields. Bernard Holtermann, a German immigrant unearthed a slab of gold seven feet high at Hill End. Holtermann became a photographer and compiled an extensive photographic record of Australian life. He employed a young English photographer, Beaufoy Merlin, to assist him and Merlin took a vast number of photographs in the settlements of Gulgong, Hill End and other nearby mining towns. He photographed almost every shop in these towns and many of the citazens. Thousands of glass negatives are preserved in the Mitchell Library, Sydney.

An elaborate sluicing arrangement on a Gippsland creek helps miners to extract gold from the river bank gravel. The wild Gippsland country was the scene of a secondary rush.

A Miners Saga

The Coolgardie safe was invented on the goldfields of Western Australia and solved the miners' problem of keeping food cool and fresh. The safe of light, perforated tin had a nay of water on the top which was connected with a damp tray underneath by strips of hessian. The water from the top tray kept the hessian sides damp and as the safe was placed in a current of air the process of evaporation lowered the temperature inside. It was only necessary to keep water in the top tray to maintain cool and fresh food.

Lasseter's Lost Reef

The legend of Lasseter's Reef began when Harold Bell Lasseter was found unconscious to the south-west of Alice Springs by an Afghan camel driver in 1897, When he had recovered, Lasseter told of a rich reef of gold which he had discovered somewhere beyond the Petermann Ranges. As proof of his claim he had with him some very promising specimens of rock. Lasseter refused to disclose the location of the reef, but tried for years to get financial backing for an expedition. Finally in the depression-ridden '30s when the lure of gold was a spur to adventurous men, subscribers put up £5,000 for an expedition, which had a truck and a plane in its equipment.

An experienced bushman, Fred Blakely, was appointed leader of the party which included a prospector, an engineer, an explorer, an air pilot and Harold Lasseter. The expedition encountered difficulties with the truck and the plane crash-landed and had to be replaced. Finally Lasseter announced that they were off course and should have been 150 miles further south.

After great hardships the party decided not to proceed, but Lasseter was determined to press on. "If I don't find the reef I'm not coming back," were his last words. Accompanied by Paul Johns, a dingo shooter, Lasseter set out with a few camels in the direction of Mount Olga. Johns was concerned about Lasseter's mental state and when Lasseter returned to camp from a short prospecting trip and said he had found his reef, Johns declared, "You are a liar." Lasseter threw some food at him and drew a revolver. There was a skirmish and the two men fought to a standstill. Johns went from the camp, leaving two camels for Lasseter's use.

In 1931 Bob Buck a Central Australian bushman, set out in search of Lasseter and found words written in the sand which indicated his fate. The camels had bolted and he was assisted for a time by Aborigines. However, his weakness and the affliction of sandy blight blindness prevented him from keeping up and he crept into a cave to die. Buck found his body. Beside it were a set of false teeth and a revolver. Nearby, beneath a tree marked with the word "dig", Buck found a tin containing some of Lasseter's papers. Other searchers have failed to find any trace of a fabulous gold reef in the central desert.

Bob Buck questions the natives.

Bobby Dazzler

A famous gold nugget was found on the Pilbara goldfield, Western Australia, in the late 19th century. It weighed over 400 ounces and was valued at £1,500. The nugget was named the "Bobby Dazzler" and this has become common Australian parlance for anything considered to have particularly high qualities.

Trouble came to the Victorian goldfields with the arrival of Chinese immigrants — often illegal immigrants marched overland from the South Australian port of Robe. Their presence on the goldfields sometimes sparked ugly racial incidents and outbursts of violence.

Scots Chinese

A Cantonese named Quong Tart who was one of the thousands of Chinese who came to the goldfields of Australia, eventually became known as one of Sydney's leading authorities on Scottish history and literature. He belonged to various Scots/Australian organisations and liked to wear kilts. Quong Tart acquired his Scottish accent on the ship coming to Australia and through working with Scottish miners at Braidwood in New South Wales. He became a successful and respected merchant in Sydney.

Kerrts Hundredweight

Doctor William John Kerr owned a sheep farming property between the Macquarie River and Neroo Creek in the Bathurst district of New South Wales. During 1851 an Aboriginal shepherd named Jemmy found several heavy, coarse stones which he reported to Doctor Kerr as having "plenty yellow". Dr. Kerr took the rock specimens to Bathurst and it was found that the total weight of gold contained in them was 106 Ibs.

Suitably aggressive looking diggers described as being "en route to deposit gold." The rifle and club are at the ready to ward off any would be thieves.

Storming of Eureka Stockade 3 December 1854, watercolour by J E Henderson.

The Rebellion At Eureka

The bloody rebellion of miners at the Eureka Stockade at Ballarat has become part of Australia's folklore as a symbol for struggle for fair play against repression and unjust laws. The rebellion in 1854 arose out of the imposition on all diggers of a licence fee of £1 a month and—a further grievance of the diggers— they could be imprisoned for not having the actual licence on them, even though their possession could be proved from the official record.

Sir Charles Hotham, who reached Victoria in June 1854 and was alarmed at the depleted state of the Treasury, ordered police to redouble their efforts to collect the fees. The comparatively quiet goldfield at Ballarat erupted on the night of 6 October when a miner named James Scobey was killed at the Eureka Hotel. The murdered man's brother accused the proprietory, Bentley, of the murder. Bentley was brought up before a magistrate and discharged.

The sorely pressed miners were indignant and called a meeting, but their belief that police sent to protect the hotel were trying to disperse the meeting led them to not. They smashed the windows and furniture and burnt the building. Police arrested three men who were sentenced to three, four and six months' imprisonment and at a further meeting on 11 November at Bakery Hill, the Ballarat Reform League was formed. A deputation of three men waited on Hotham to demand the release of the prisoners but he had already sent additional troops to Ballarat and on 27 November refused the petition.

The troops arrived in Ballarat with fixed bayonets. Their captain's refusal to treat with the rebels fired the crowd, who threw itself on the convoy, overturned a wagon, captured another and injured three or four soldiers. This action was condemned by the leaders of the Reform League, but a meeting of its Committee proposed the burning of the obnoxious licences. Bonfires were lighted and the licences burned there and then. The next day, 30 November, the police were ordered to make a specially vigorous licence hunt. A squadron of mounted troopers was received with a volley of stones and the occasional pistol shot. Commissioner Rede endeavoured to read the Riot Act, but was told the licences were all burned and that if he liked the whole camp of Ballarat would surrender—an obviously absurd proposal as it would have been impossible to guard so many prisoners.

Peter Lalor was elected leader of the Reform League and under a blue flag adorned with the star of the Southern Cross. The assembled diggers swore "to stand truly by each other and to fight to defend our rights and liberties". An area of about an acre on the Eureka claim was enclosed with piled up mining slabs, building timber and other material handy. On 3 December, Sunday moming, when the population of the Stockade was depleted as many men had left to forage for food at about 4.30 a.m., a troop of 276 men were marched silently to the Stockade. Many of the miners were asleep when a signal gun was fired and a storming party of 64 rushed the Stockade.

In the first volley several men fell on both sides, but the line of advancing bayonets, flanked on both sides by cavalry and mounted police, was too much for the diggers. They turned to seek shelter and it was all over. Of the military force, Captain Wise and four privates were killed and about a dozen injured. Sixteen miners were killed and at least eight others died of their wounds. A total of 114 prisoners were taken, but all were discharged except 13 who were held to stand trial for high treason. Lalor, badly wounded, managed to escape.

Ballarat was put under martial law and on 5 December Sir Robert Nickle arrived with reinforcements. He listened to the miners' grievances and his conciliatory treatment helped to calm down the agitation, as did his announcement that the Governor had appointed a commission to enquire into the miners' grievances. In subsequent trials all the men arrested were acquitted.

Peter Lalor survived a number of ordeals while fleeing from the police, but was subsequently pardoned and was elected to the Victorian Parliament in 1855. He remained a Member for 32 years. The story of Eureka is told in these verses by Victor Daley, first printed in 1901.

The reward poster for the arrest of the Eureka leaders, Peter lalor and George Black.

Peter Lalor—Eureka hero.

On the goldfields at Kalgoorlie in 1894. The miners of this rush endured extreme hardship in semi-desert conditions. Water had to be transported to the fields and camel trains were often used for this purpose.

The Rebel Flag

The miners who rebelled over the licence fees and fought Governor Sir Charles Hotham's troopers at the Eureka Stockade in 1854 hoisted a flag The Southern Cross. Rafaello Carboni in his book The Eureka Stockade described it "The Southern Cross was hoisted up the flag staff—a very splendid pole, 80 feet in length, and straight as an arrow. This made an appearance of our standard, in the midst of armed men, sturdy, hard working gold diggers of all languages and colours, was a fascinating object to Ballarat miners, first hoisted on the old spot Bakery Hill. The flag is silk, blue ground, with a large silver cross, similar to the one in our southern firmament: no device of arms, but all exceedingly chaste and natural."

The Whip Hand

Lola Montez was the darling of the Australian goldfields in the 1850s. Her real name was Delores Eliza Gilbert, an Irish adventuress who had been a lover of the composer Liszt and of King Louis of Bavaria who made her the Countess of Landsfeld and lost his throne because of her proposed reforms in his country. She presented to the miners a frenetic stage show based on Bavarian history—performed with such spirit, rather than accuracy or sense, that it gave the miners a rousing night out. She was criticised by the Editor of the Ballarat Times. Erle Seekamp, and retaliated by announcing from the stage that he was "a little fond of drinking". Seekamp replied in the Times "Please for a 'little' substitute 'very' because I can carry my three bottles with any bishop in Christendom." Lola Montez encountered Seekamp in the bar of the United States Hotel and attacked him with a whip. Seekamp, not to be outdone, returned the next night and struck back with a heavier whip.

People & Places

Opening of the Parliament of Commonwealth of Australia, Melbourne, May 9, 1901 by King George V.

Nationalism

The sneering reference by the English to Australians as Antipodeans caused indignation among many citizens. The poet Bernard O'Dowd gave expression to such feelings with the following:

ANTIPODEANS

Antipodean? Whew! We are the head, The oceanic head, while you, slung low with lands that scrape the floor of heaven, gaze Far o'er the Bull your old Europa wed Up to the Chambers of the South where glow Our pennant stars, our wider Milky Ways.

Father of Federation

Sir Henry Parkes, the Premier of New South Wales for 19 years from 1872-1891, is considered to be the father of Federation. He predicted a "more permanent Federal understanding" as early as 1867, but an after-dinner speech at Tenterfield in 1889 was a powerful, emotional appeal on behalf of Federation and similar speeches throughout New South Wales resulted in the unsuccessful Federal conference in Melbourne in 1890. Parkes was present at the 1891 national convention, but he disapproved of the draft constitution. A meeting in 1893 adopted his suggestion that a convention be elected to draw up a constitution, but this convention marked the beginning of steps towards the achievement of Federation in 1900. Parkes had been a toy maker, a labourer, and journalist and newspaper owner before he was elected to the New South Wales Legislative Council in 1854. Evidence of his serious emotional attachment to Federation can be seen in his poem The Australian Flag.

THE AUSTRALIAN FLAG

Fling out the flag—our virgin flag,
Which foeman's shot has never rent,
And plant it high on mount and crag,
O'er busy town and lonely tent.

Where commerce rears her stately halls,
And where the miner rends the rock,
Where the sweet rain on cornfields falls,
Where pastures feed the herd and flock.

Still let it float o'er homes of peace,
Our starry cross—our glorious sign!
While Nature's bounteous gifts increase,
And freedom's glories brighter shine.

Brave hearts may beat in labour's strife,
They need no spur of martial pride;
High deeds may crown a gentle life,
And spread their radiance far and wide.

Fling out the flag—and guard it well!—
O'er pleasant fields the foe ne'er trod;
Long may our guardian heroes dwell
In league with truth—in camp with God!

In other lands the patriot boasts
His standard borne through slaughter's flood,
Which, waving o'er infuriate hosts,
Was consecrate in fire and blood.

A truer charm our flag endears;
Where'er it waves, on land or sea,
It bears no stain of blood and tears—
Its glory is its purity.

SIR HENRY PARKES

The Larrikin Pushes

The Australian larrikin of the 19th century was a tough street-wise character; always ready for a fight or some illegal devilment. He moved in gangs or "pushes", was contemptuous of the ordinary citizen and his enemy was the law. The word is believed to have had its origin in the Scottish pronunciation of the word "larking" by a Melbourne police sergeant. To the question from a magistrate: "What was the accused up to sergeant?" he would reply, "Just larrikin your worship."

Edward Kinglade in his book The Australian at Home published in 1891, provides this description of a larrikin:

PORTRAIT OF THE LARRIKIN

Let me give you a description of a typical male specimen as he may be found at the street corners about seven o'clock in the evening, expectorating tobacco juice and talking blasphemy. He is generally a weedy youth, undersized and slight, but like all Australians, who are cast in a lanky not thickset mould, he is wiry and active. He has a repulsive face, low forehead, small eyes, a colourless skin, and irregular discoloured teeth. His hat is either small, round and hard, or a black slouch. He pays attention to his dress, which is always of dark colour and very tight-fitting, the coat of the shortest, the trousers like fleshings, and his boots very high-heeled and small, the impress of every toe being clearly distinguishable en repousse.

Knots of these creatures collect in the evening, and the streets are not the more pleasant to walk in for their presence. They call themselves "pushes", and there are often conflicts between those who infect different parts of the town. The larrikin is a coward. He is only courageous when there are numbers present, and he prefers his adversary in a minority of one to ten, or thereabouts.

Throwing lumps of blue metal is one of his favourite modes of attack. The agility with which he will discharge his missile and then dart around the nearest corner to avoid the return shot is wonderful.

W. T. Goodge in his poem The Great Australian Slanguage of 1897 describes the larrikin's mode of speech, so well employed in C. J. Dennis' classic poem, The Sentimental Bloke.

LARRIKIN LANGUAGE

Tis the everyday Australian
Has a language of his own,
Has a language, or a slanguage,
Which can simply stand alone.
And a "dickin pitch to kid us"
Is a synonym for"lie",
And to "nark it" means to stop it,
And to "nit it" means to fly!

And a bosom friend's a "cobber",
And a horse a "prad" or "moke",
While a casual acquaintance
Is a "joker" or a "bloke",
And his ladylove's his "donah",
Or his "clinah" or his "tarf',
Or his "little bit o' muslin",
As it used to be his "bart".
And his naming of the coinage,
Is a mystery to some,
With his "quid" and "half-a-caser"
And his "deener" and his "scrum".
And a "tin-back" is a party
Who's remarkable for luck,
And his food is called his "tucker"
Or his "panem" or his "chuck".

A policeman is a "johnny"
Or a "copman" or a "trap",
And a thing obtained on credit
Is invariably"strap".
A conviction's known as "trouble",
And a gaol is called a "jug",
And a sharper is a "spieler"
And a simpleton's a ' tug".

If he hits a man in fighting
That is what he calls a "plug",
If he borrows money from you
He will say he "bit your lug".

And to "shake it" is to steal it,
And to "strike it" is to beg;
And a jest is "poking borak",
And a jester "pulls your leg".

Things are "crook" when they go wrongly
In the language of the "push",
But when things go as he wants 'em
He declares it is "all cush".
When he's bright he's got a "napper",
And he's "ratty" when he's daft,
And when looking for employment
He is "out o' blooming graft".

And his clothes he calls his "clobber"
Or his "togs", but what of that
When a "castor" or a "kady"
Is the name he gives his hat!
And our undiluted English
Is a fad to which we cling,
But the great Australian slanguage
Is a truly awful thing!

W. T. GOODGE

Larrikin land The home of the Sydney "pushes" were the tenements of The Rocks, Redfern and Paddington in old Sydney. They spilled into the streets at night to indulge in gangfights, thuggery and general public mayhem.

Inventive Explorer

The explorer, Major Thomas Mitchell, is credited with having introduced the canvas waterbag. During his expedition in south-western Queensland, Mitchell broke his water-bottle. As an experiment he sewed pieces of canvas together to make a bag which he greased with tallow. Before the introduction of the waterbag, goat and sheepskin water containers were widely used by settlers and travellers.

Old Bell

A bell which peals at St. Augustine's Church of England at Hamilton in Brisbane is said to be one of the oldest bells in the world. The ancient bell first hung in a Rumanian Church in 320 AD. and was there until 1918, when the church was shelled. British soldiers rescued the bell and buried it in the sand at Varna on the Black Sea coast. A group of merchant seamen from the ship Melara unearthed the treasure and later presented it to Captain Campbell Thompson of Brisbane who in turn presented it to St. Augustine's Church.

Strange Sounding Names

There are a number of, mostly unprovable, stories of how some peculiar place names in Australia had their origins. On the south coast of New South Wales the village of Whipstick was named because teamsters cut whip handles there. They could walk a few yards off the road and select whip handles from saplings growing in the bush.

Adavale in Queensland was originally known as Ada's Veil. It was named by one of the early settlers in the district whose wife Ada had lost her veil there. When the railway came to the town its name was changed to Adavale.

Queensland's shortest name place is OK. It is said to have been named after an empty jam tin bearing that brand by a miner who was sinking a shaft.

The town of Limpinwood on the New South Wales-Queensland border commemorates an old time carrier, known as "Hopping Jack" Wood. He and other carriers camped at the same place regularly and a store was built there which started the town of Hopping Wood. This was later changed to Limping Wood.

The little town of Cape Clear about 40 miles south of Ballarat in Victoria was so called because a teamster was bogged there and erected a notice as a warning to others. His "keep clear" sign read "Kape Klear" and this gradually evolved into Cape Clear.

The Victorian Government Surveyor, J. G. Wilmot, named some districts in a highly personal fashion. He was alluding to a love affair of two young ladies, Laura and Helen, with the same man. The question was, "Will Laura or Helen do it?" Wilmot named a district Willaura and a nearby locality Hellendoit. He also named the district of Miepoll after an identity of the district who was always quoting his wife, "My Poll said this" or "My Poll did this".

The Victorian town of Katamitte is suggested to have been named because one of the earliest settlers would turn to his wife and say, "Kate, am I tight?" after they had been drinking in company.

King George's Sound in Western Australia has a bay known as Two People Bay, a reef known as The Drunken Sailor and an island called Mistaken Island. Two People Bay is said to have been named after an American and a French naval ship sought refuge in the bay together. Mistaken Island was once called Rabbit Island but when early settlers discovered that the "rabbit holes" that they saw across the bay were penguins' burrows they changed the name to Mistaken Island. The Drunken Sailor was so called because a drunken helmsman had steered a ship onto the reef.

The Queensland district of Struckoil was named after a play Struckoil which was a great success in Australia for J. C. Williamson and his wife, Maggie Moore. Some prospectors who had come to Mount Morgan to register a gold mine saw the play and when introduced to Maggie Moore, they decided to call their mine "Struckoil".

Bennelong Point, the site of the Sydney Opera House, is named after an Aborigine who acted as a go-between for Arthur Phillip with the natives who lived around Port Jackson. When Phillip returned to England he took Bennelong and another Aborigine with him. They were presented to King George III and achieved the status of celebrities. Bennelong returned to Australia with Phillip's successor, Captain John Hunter.

The Victorian goldfields town of Bendigo was named after an English prize fighter, William Thompson, who was popularly known as Bendigo after one of his christian names of Abendego. The official name of the district became Sandhurst, but Bendigo remained in such usage that the authorities were forced to revert to the original name.

The Lochard Gorge near Port Campbell on the rugged south-westem coast of Victoria was named after the wreck of the vessel Lochard. There were only two survivors, a cadet Tom Pierce and a girl Eva Carmichael. Pierce dragged Eva by the hair through the surf to a safe part of the shore and, leaving her in a cave at the foot of the gorge, he climbed the cliffs and got help.

The Ruined City

The ruined city of Arnhem Land is an unusual expanse of sandstone near the Phelp River, Northern Territory, about 300 miles east of Darwin. It has been described as one of the wonders of the world and is a repository for some superb examples of Aboriginal rock paintings and carvings.

Battle Of Rothbury

The Battle of Rothbury was a serious clash between police and coalminers at the town of Rothbury, New South Wales, on 16 December 1929. One miner was killed, nine others received bullet wounds and 43 suffered other injuries. As a prelude to the battle earlier that year 10,000 miners received dismissal notices at 27 collieries owned by the Northern Colliery Owners Association. They had refused to accept a reduction of 12 1/2 percent in contract rates and a shilling a shift for those on wages. They were then locked out of the mines. The Rothbury fracas occurred after 6,000 miners marched in protest against the use of scab labour underground.

Missing Mace

An unusual Royal Commission was held in Melbourne in the 1890s to try and unravel the mystery of the missing mace. The mace disappeared from the Legislative Assembly overnight and was not seen again. There were rumours that it was taken to a party of Parliamentarians as the centre piece of a mock Parliament but the Royal Commission uncovered no evidence of this. The silver mace, with a gold coating, was valued at £300 and a Government offer of £100 reward failed to clear up the mystery of the loss of the greatest symbol of Parliament.

Cooee

"Cooee", an Aboriginal word meaning "come here", is often used as a call in bush or out-back areas. The call, because of its penetration, was used as a means of attracting attention in timbered country or for trying to locate someone who was lost.

Worst Flood

Australia's most disastrous flood occurred at Gundagai on 23 June 1852. It caused much of the town to be washed away and the loss of 74 lives. There had been torrential rain before the disaster and the Murrumbidgee had been rising steadily, but the townspeople were unaware of the danger. During the night the river broke its banks and swept through the town with a vast wave, pushing debris before it. People awoke to find muddy waters swirling through their homes, and houses collapsed and were swept away. Through the night men, women and children clung to trees and roof tops while horses, cattle and people swept past them, struggling for refuge. The morning revealed hundreds of people clinging to trees and many were there for days before they were rescued.

Royal Rampage

Australia's first royal visitor was Queen Victoria's second son, Prince Alfred, the Duke of Edinburgh, who came to Australia in 1867 as a naval officer in command of the steam frigate

Galatea. Melbourne spent a quarter of a million pounds on his welcome and a public feast on the Yarra attracted 60,000 citizens. The Duke was advised not to appear and the angry citizens eventually rampaged through the long tables of food and filled buckets with Colonial wine from an elevated vat which was to have been fed into a fountain turned on by the Duke. The Duke was wise not to attend, because at a picnic in Sydney he was wounded in the back by a pistol shot from an Irishman, who was later hanged for attempted murder.

The Impressionists

Tom Roberts was known as the father of Australian Impressionism, a revolution in Australian painting which followed his return from painting in England, France and Spain in 1885. On his return to Melbourne he described the principles of Impressionism to two other great names in Australian art, Arthur Streeton and Charles Conder. They were the leading figures in the Heidelberg School which had, as its aim, painting in the open air and natural impressions of the Australian light and landscape. Their painting coincided with and complemented a wave of nationalism that was also reflected in Australian literature. Roberts' best known subjects, which gave a heroic impression of Australian bush life, were The Golden Fleece, A Mountain Muster, Shearing The Rams, and The Breakaway.

A Long Line

To bring Australia in touch with the outside world an overland telegraph of 1,800 miles had to be built from Port Augusta in South Australia to Darwin. The line took 23 months to build and required 36,000 telegraph poles and a vast logistical backup to supply the contractors with food and sustenance in the desert. A herd of several thousand sheep and cattle had to be kept to provide food for the workers.

High Jinks

Ever eager for sensation, the people of Sydney turned out in force in April 1877 to watch a 27-year-old, Mr H. L' Estrange, walk across Middle Harbour on a tightrope 340 feet above the water. The rope was stretched between two cliffs 1,420 feet apart Halfway across, L' Estrange stood on one leg, lay on his back and sat down and surveyed the cheering onlookers with a small telescope. L' Estrange, carrying a 60 lb. balancing pole, completed the crossing in 10 minutes.

Not To Knight

In the wave of nationalism of the late 19th century, many leading Australians felt that the conferring of knighthoods on them would compromise their independence in dealing with Great Britain. The Premier of Victoria, Duncan Gillies, and the Chief Secretary, Alfred Deakin, who was later to become the Prime Minister of the Commonwealth, refused knighthoods when they were offered them at the first Imperial Conference in London in 1887. Peter Lalor, the hero of the Eureka Stockade, also refused a knighthood.

Deakin wrote to his wife, "Your chance of being Lady Deakin has been thrown away by your loving husband. To have declined the honour at 30 years of age is not perhaps remarkable, but having the offer so early is another instance of my marvellous fortune in public affairs."

The Lagerphone

A popular instrument in early Australia was the lagerphone which could provide any rhythm base for an impromptu musical evening. The lagerphone was made by removing the cork from about three hundred bottle tops and piercing them by driving a nail through the centre. Smaller nails were then used to attach the bottle top loosely to a broomstick. A rubber tip at the bottom end provided the bounce and a hand grip at the top enabled the player to bounce the lagerphone to any desired rhythm and achieve the effect of tambourines. A metal stick hit against a cleared space on the lagerphone added to the rhythmic possibilities.

The Fish And Chips

The Blue Mountains express running between Sydney and the Blue Mountains became known as The Fish in the 1860s because the driver Jock Heron, with his name corrupted to Herring, was nicknamed the Big Fish. The second division of the train became known as the Chips.

Box Hill Messiah

James Cowley Morgan Fisher lived in the Box Hill district of Melbourne. In the late 1860s he decided that he was the Messiah and gathered a band of followers. The Fisherites

Opening of the new Theatre Royal, Sydney. (Illustrated Sydney News 12 January 1876)

Early Actors

An actor who was a sensational success with Australian audiences was the Englishman, Gustavus V. Brooke, who made his Australian debut in 1855 as Othello and adapted himself easily to Shakespearian or light comedy roles. He toured the goldfields and was prepared to play before an audience in a pub if there was no theatre. The diggers threw nuggets to him and in Melbourne he was given a gold cup and salver and a gold statuette of Shakespeare. In Sydney he received a silver candelabrum. He was returning to Australia by popular demand in 1866 when his ship, The London, sank in the Bay of Biscay and he was drowned. As the few survivors pulled away from the sinking vessel in their boat, Brooke called to them, "Remember me to my friends in Melbourne".

Another famous actor who visited Australia in 1855 was the American, Edwin Booth who was the brother of John Wilkes Booth, the actor who assassinated President Lincoln in 1865. Booth visited Australia in 1855 and was acclaimed for his Shakespearian roles.

were described by Ivan Southall in his book A Tale of Box Hill published in 1957, as: "Some 50 men and women of eccentric habit and cast-iron virtue. James Cowley Morgan Fisher was a magnificent specimen, over six feet tall with the features of a Greek God, the shoulders of a giant and a flowing mane of white hair. His beard too, was long and white and his eyes were pools of power. He taught his flock the ten commandments, he interpreted Mosaic law in all its mystery, magnificence and beauty." Southall tells this story of Fisher: "Legend said that Fisher took his people to Blackburn Lake to pray while he worked a miracle. 'Do you believe?' he boomed from the shore. 'Have you the faith that I can walk upon the waters?' 'Hallelujah,' they cried. 'We believe.' Fisher raised his eyes to heaven, 'Then I have no need to do it'." Fisherites were a polygamist sect and Fisher himself had three sisters as his wives.

Hero Of The Skies

Sir Charles Kingsford Smith (1897-1935) and Charles Ulm, with a crew of two Americans, made the first flight across the Pacific in the Southern Cross in 1928. Smith had a remarkable flying career and became a celebrated figure in Australia. After serving with the Royal Flying Corps in World War I he became one of six pilots of the first Australian Airway Company— Western Australian Airways— and flew with them for two years.

With Ulm he made a round-Australia flight in June 1927 and, after his crossing of the Pacific, he flew non-stop from Point Cook, Victoria, to Perth and made the first successful crossing of the Tasman Sea with Ulm. While en route to England in 1929 his plane was forced down in the Kimberleys and was not found for 12 days. Two men lost their lives and the incident became known as the Coffee Royal Affair, but Kingsford Smith and Ulm were exonerated in a public enquiry.

With Ulm, Lichfield and McWilliams, he flew from Australia to England in 12 days, 18 hours to set a new record in June 1929 and in October 1930 he flew from England to Darwin solo in nine days, 22 1/2 hours. Smith established a passenger service between Brisbane and Sydney, Melbourne and Hobart but the loss of the Southern Cloud in the Southern Alps of New South Wales caused a widespread fear of air travel and the company closed down in 1931. In October 1935 he attempted to fly from England to Australia with J. T. Pethybridge but the plane, The Lady Southern Cross, was lost without trace somewhere over Burma.

King Of Bass Strait

James Munroe lived for more than 30 years on Preservation Island in the Bass Strait and his control over the islanders was so great that he became their uncrowned chieftain and was known as The King of the Eastern Straits. He would call the islanders into conference, give them orders and settle their disputes. When he died in January 1845, aged 82, he left three Aboriginal wives and many children. Munroe lived by cultivating vegetables, which he bartered to visiting sealers for goods they brought to him.

Sing'Em Muck

Dame Nellie Melba gained public notoriety when the life story of the well- known singer Dame Clara Butt was published in 1928. The book quoted Melba as saying: "So you are going to Australia Well, I made twenty thousand pounds on my tour there, but of course that will never be done again. It's a wonderful country, and you'll have a good time. What are you going to sing? All I can say is—sing 'em muck! It's all they can understand!" When the book was published Madam Melba publicly stated that she had never used the words and threatened the publishers and the author, Mrs. Winifred Ponder. The publisher removed the offending paragraphs from copies withdrawn from sale, but the phrase "sing 'em muck" remained attributed to Melba and she could not shake it off.

Sir Charles Kingsford Smith Australia's most famous pioneer aviator. He created a number of flight records between 1927 and 1935 when his plane was lost over Burma.

A Little Heroine

The heroinism of Jane Duff; aged seven, who used most of her clothing to protect her brothers from the cold when they became lost in the bush in 1864, became a household tale in early Australia. The Duff children, Isaac, nine, Jane, and Frank, four and a half, were children of a station worker and became lost in wild bush country near Goroke in western Victoria. A search party led by a black tracker named Dick-a-Dick found the children alive but very weak some nine days after they were lost. They had eaten only quandongs, a wild fruit. S. T. Gill commemorated the incident with a painting and the story was retold in L. J. Blake's Lost in thc Bush.

Much Married Bishop

The Catholic Vicar of Darwin earlier this century was a French missionary, Francis Xavier Gsell. He had a territory of half a million square miles and became known as "the Bishop with a 150 wives," because of his practice of purchasing native girls from their families so that they became, by tribal law, his own wives. He was then able to arrange marriages for many of them to young men of the Christian faith, thus getting round the tribal custom of marrying young girls to elders of the tribe.

A Tribal Ruler

Robert Joel Cooper, better known in the north as King Joe, became the absolute ruler of a tribe of Aborigines at Melville Island, northern Australia. Cooper arrived in the Northern Territory in 1881 having come overland from South Australia. He soon won over the fierce Melville Islanders and was proclaimed chief over the five tribes. He was put through all the secret rites of the Aborigines and to the day of his death never revealed them to another white man.

Cooper was a man of commanding appearance and of principle. He was a nonsmoker and a teetotaller with strong moral convictions, and the warlike Aborigines of Melville Island respected and obeyed his rule completely. He attended personally to the punishment of the evil doers, wearing only a loin cloth and taking a spear, woomera and throwing stick to hunt down any Aborigine who had broken one of the tribal laws and had fled to escape punishment. A fine tracker and bushman, he always returned with the offender.

Once, two native contenders to chieftainship challenged him to combat. Cooper accepted their challenge and prepared for a battle in which he was to fight both men in turn. Before hundreds of natives he and his first opponent faced each other in loin cloths, carrying only spears and woomeras. Their contest with spears ended in stalemate as they were both too skilled, so the elders of the tribes decided they should fight with waddies. After a fierce fight Cooper got a home blow to his opponent's skull and knocked him unconscious. The following day the second challenger could not withstand the trial by spear and was wounded in the left thigh and King Joe had re-established himself in power. Cooper could speak many Aboriginal dialects and travelled widely between Darwin and the Gulf of Carpenteria. He made his living as a buffalo shooter and is said to have accounted for 27,000 buffaloes.

The Tichborne Case

One of Australia's most audacious hoaxes involved Arthur Orton, a butcher from Wagga Wagga, who posed as Roger Charles Doughty Tichborne who was the missing heir to a baronetcy and a fortune. While Tichborne was slim and well-educated, Orton was 25 stone and almost illiterate, but he represented himself as her son to Lady Tichborne and she accepted that he was her long-lost child. Orton brought an action against the Trustees of the Estate in 1871, and claimed an income of £15,000 a year, but he lost the case and was subsequently found guilty of perjury and imprisoned for 14 years.

Early Aborigines of NSW, published 1798.

A Tragic Hero

The life of Adam Lindsay Gordon, mounted policeman, horse-breaker, remittance man, Parliamentarian, stable-owner, jockey and poet, ended in tragedy when he suicided on the eve of the publication of his best known book of verse Bush Ballads and Galloping Rhymes.

Gordon was a redoubtable horseman. He created a record at Flemington on 10 October 1869 by winning three steeplechases in one afternoon, two of them on his own horses. He achieved an amazing feat of horsemanship that nearly cost him his life. In the late 1860s, when he was living in the Mount Gambier district of South Australia, he was riding with a party of friends and they began to play follow-the leader, with Gordon setting the pace and leading the others over formidable obstacles.

"Well, damn well follow me now!" shouted Gordon, and he galloped his horse towards a high post and rail fence behind which was a six foot ledge and then a drop off to rocks bordering the Blue Lake. Gordon's mount cleared the fence, turned in midair, and came to a standstill on the ledge, only inches from death. Gordon's leap was repeated in 1896 by champion buck jumper, athlete and author Lance Skuthorpe. who made the leap for a £10 bet

After Gordon's death the poet Henry Kendall, composed this memorial ode:

ADAM LINDSAY GORDON

A Memorial Ode

At rest! Hard by the margin of that sea
Whose sounds are mingled with his noble verse
Now lies the shell that never more will house
The fine strong spirit of my gifted friend.
Yea, he who flashed upon us suddenly
A shining soul with syllables of fire,
Who sang the first great songs these lands can claim
To be their own; the one who did not seem
To know what royal place awaited him
Within the Temple of the Beautiful,
Has passed away; and we who knew him sit
Aghast in darkness, dumb with that great grief
Whose stature yet we cannot comprehend;
While over yonder churchyard, hearsed With pines.
The night wind sings its immemorial hymn.
And sobs above a newly-covered grave.
The bard, the scholar, and the man who lived
That frank, that open-hearted life which keeps
The splendid fire of English chivalry
From dying out the one who never wronged
A fellow man; the faithful friend Who judged
The many, anxious to be loved of him,
By what he saw, and not by what he heard,
As lesser spirits do; the brave, great soul
That never told a lie, or turned aside
To fly from danger—he, as I say, was one
Of that bright company this sin-stained world
Can ill afford to lose.
They did not know.
The hundreds who had read his sturdy verse
And revelled over ringing major notes,
The mournful meaning of the undersong
Which runs through al1 he wrote, and often takes
The deep autumnal, half-prophetic tone
Of forest winds in March; nor did they think
That on that healthy-hearted man there lay
The wild specific curse which seems to cling
For ever to the Poet's twofold life!
To Adam Lindsay Gordon, I who laid
Two years ago on Lionel Michael's grave
A tender leaf of my regard. yea,
I Who culled a garland from the flowers of song
To place where Harpur sleeps; I, left alone,
The sad disciple of a shining band,
Now gone — to Adam Lindsay Gordon's name
I dedicate these lines; and if 'tis true
That past the darkness of the grave, the soul
Becomes omniscient, then the bard may stoop
From his high seat to take the offering
And read it with a sigh for human friends,
In human bonds, and grey with human griefs.
And having wove and proffered this poor wreath,
I stand to-day as lone as he who saw
At nightfall, through the glimmering moony mist
The last of Arthur on the wailing mere,
And strained in vain to hear the going voice.

HENRY KENDAL

The Big Apple

There are conflicting stories of how the famous Granny Smith apple was discovered but it was grown on the farm of Mrs. Maria Smith who came to Australia from England in the early 1800s and established, with her husband Thomas and two sons, a farm at what is now Eastwood, about 12 miles from Sydney.

The Smiths' established an orchard and Granny Smith took a stall in the city markets. Some versions of the beginning of the Granny Smith apple are as follows: Mr. Smith brought home some fruit cases from the markets and in the bottom of one were the remains of some Tasmanian apples known as French Crabs. Mrs. Smith emptied it onto a bank of the creek which ran past her farm and eventually a tree grew there with apples which were different from any other. The tree was given special attention and by budding and grafting Granny Smith soon had quite a large orchard of these special trees. The fruit from them was packed separately and brought higher prices in the markets than any other apples. The case was labelled "apples from Granny Smith", but this was soon abbreviated to "Granny Smith".

Another suggestion is that she was peeling the Tasmanian apples at her kitchen window and threw the skin and the cores out onto a flower bed. It is suggested that the strain came from a sport— a bud and branch which produced fruit different from that on the rest of the tree—or a seedling which created fruit different from the apple whose seeds were planted. Unfortunately, the property was sub-divided and the famous parent tree grubbed out to make way for suburbia. The Granny Smith apple tree is now grown in many countries.

The Flying Pieman

A remarkable and extraordinarily athletic eccentric of early Sydney was the Flying Pieman, William Francis King, who migrated to Australia from England in 1829 and became a travelling pie vendor to sporting contests and in the streets of Sydney. Around 1845, when he was 38 years old, the pieman began to achieve great athletic feats. To the astonishment of Sydney citizens he walked 1,634 miles in five weeks and four days.

He walked from the obelisk in Macquarie Place, Sydney, to the 16 mile stone at Parramatta and back in six hours. He walked from Sydney to Parramatta and back twice a day for six consecutive days. He walked from Parramatta Church to the Church at Windsor on three successive days, taking around eight hours each day for the journey of 431/2 miles.

He undertook to walk from Campbelltown to Sydney between 9.30 at night and 8.40 the next morning carrying a dog weighing around 70 Ibs., and he arrived 20 minutes before the allotted time. According to Randolph Bedford in his book Nought to 33, "He carried a sheep to and from Parramatta and on his return to Sydney slaughtered the sheep, baked the mutton and sold the pies at high prices. He had to get the limelight somehow and he got it by arduous methods of doing the unnecessary."

An Australian Heroine

An early Australian heroine was Grace Bussell, the 16-year old daughter of a Western Australian station owner. The Georgette was run on a sand bank near the Margaret River on 30 November 1876. When she heard of the disaster, Grace Bussell mounted her horse and dashed to the beach. With a rope attached to her horse she was able to tow the passengers ashore in groups. W. B. Kimberley in his History of Western Australia says. ' Her words of hope cheered many who were hard beset and for a time when her horse's legs became entangled in a rope she was in danger of drowning. She was awarded the Humane Society medal and a watch from the British Government."

Tales Of Henry Lawson

Henry Lawson was a great ill-starred figure of Australian literature. With his genius for capturing the language, the plain and simple heroism of bush life, and his ability to tell dramatic stories of ordinary people, he won a following throughout Australia — a following that perhaps reflected an emerging national pride and a recognition of the uniqueness of the Australian character. Yet Lawson was a tragic and lonely figure, often broke and cadging a loan from friends, often ignored or belittled by critics, with a ruined family life, a hopeless addiction to alcohol and an increasing deafness which isolated him from his fellow men. Although much has been written on Lawson one view by historian Manning Clark, indicates the depth of his personal suffering.

Manning Clark On Lawson

He wanted more than the sympathy of a woman. He wanted to know what had gone wrong and why it had all happened to him He played with the idea that it had all been wrong from the start, that he was the plaything of the past, that there was gypsy blood in his veins, that he had been suckled by an Aborigine He played with the idea that he was the victim of some malign spirit in the world. He tried all sorts of cures. He tried the doctors, but they could only tell him what he knew already, namely, that he should stop. He tried hypnotism, but that only ended in a farce, or rather with him having once again to joke about the great agony in his life. "How will you take me," he asked the long-suffering George Robertson in February 1905, "hypnotized or tight?" He became like a man who had escaped into another world, from which, from time to time, he sent back frantic appeals for help, chiefly financial help. "I want that quid" he used to say to George Robertson. Once he commanded George Robertson to send round ambassadors to discuss the "quid" owed to him by the firm, but then added the postscript not to send the ambassadors straight away as everyone in his place was "very tight". When George Robertson made him yet another advance against future work knowing full well where most of that would be squandered— Robertson himself being a high- minded Presbyterian— Lawson in gratitude would send him the briefest of replies: "You are a man." He used the same direct approach to the theatrical entrepreneur, Bland Holt "I want that quid—pound (otherwise four casers) tonight I will wait. Yours faithlessly, Henry Lawson." He added the postscript "I am straight".

To raise money for drinking he gave assurances he knew to be untrue. What was worse he knew the recipients knew the assurances were false. 'I will not drink it," he would tell Bland Holt or George Robertson. They must not make hurtful charges against him. "You hurt me a lot" he told Bland Holt in June 1906. For he was still a vunerable man. To make life bearable at all, in addition to the anaesthetic of alcohol, he had to indulge in verbal clowning so that those with whom he was risking some sort of human contact would have their attention distracted from peering into him, that being one of the many things he would not tolerate. He wanted them to think of Henry Lawson not as a wreck, or a man who had brought himself to destruction, but as a superb wit. In correspondence with friends he would sign himself under some title such as Vice-President of The Ancient-Order of Sinners — softening the selflaceration with a witticism habitually punishing and preening himself at one and the same time. Nothing could stop the career downhill. The drinking was always accompanied by extravagant shouting for other thirsty men around the great Australian communion rail. As he had shown in that marvellous story Telling Mrs Baker that was how men of his temperament behaved. This meant there was little if any money left to pay the grocer's bills and the rent, let alone that maintenance money of two pounds a week to Bertha. In desperation, all her written appeals to him having led to naught she finally decided in April 1905 to charge him with wife desertion. That led to him being lodged in Darlinghurst Gaol. There he appealed to David Scott Mitchell, the man who had helped him travel to London, for a loan to enable him to get out of gaol "I have been drinkinq lately," he confessed, "but I never ill-treated my wife " With

Henry Lawson in the 1890's.

the financial help provided by Mitchell he was released from custody the following day

Not even that humiliation and suffering could halt for long his rush downhill. To the dismay of those who loved him, cherished him and treasured him as one of the few writers who had fashioned Australian national sentiment, he was talking far too much about death for a man of' only forty years. He was fond of telling his friends Waverley Cemetery was becoming so overcrowded that there were few grave sites left — and he was following shortly. He was much given to horse-play and slapstick humour He was kicked out of Jimmy Edmond's office in the city of Sydney for singing drunkenly the words

We love thee for thy beauty
But 'tis not for that alone

For ever since his Bohemian days in the 1890s he loved to epater les bouryeois With a double entendre.

When the evil spirit was upon him, and he became a victim to the ravages of the "monster" he issued an I. O. U. to any man standing round the bar who was prepared to lend him a bob or two, all that he needed for the agony within to disappear. For nature had not only played the cruel joke of planting in him an irresistible craving, but also a chemistry of the body which meant he disintegrated after one glass of beer. There were also those ungovernable rages. He,

A settlers hut in Gippsland Victoria.

the gentlest of men, the man with the eyes of "haunting sympathy' could change suddenly, and quite inexplicably, into a violent and murderous monster. The man who preached about "the cup of kindness" and tramping "in mateship side by side" occasionally poured out a stream of abuse and hatred for those who had hurt him. Once he burst into the offices of the Bulletin in George Street brandishing his walking-stick, which in his rage he had converted into an Irish shelalgh. He smashed windows. threatened to push down doors while shouting out loud what he would do to A. G. Stephens once he laid hands on him. Then he wlthdrew, the storm was over. and he retired to the haven of that "good little woman" Isabel Byers. the one whose patience was inexhaustible.

Under the influence of such behaviour the appearance of the man began to change. He began to lose much of' the innocent face which had caused other eyes to gape in unbelief that there could be such a vunerable person, when he first came down to Sydney in 1886.

From *In Search of Henry Lawson (Macmillan)*

Two of Henry Lawson's well known works, his poem Andy's Gone With Cattle and his short story The Drover's Wife demonstrate the power and haunting quality of his work.

ANDY'S GONE WITH CATTLE

Our Andy's gone with cattle now —
Our hearts are out of order —
With drought he's gone to battle now
Across the Queensland border.

He's left us in dejection now;
Our thoughts with him are roving;
It's dull on this selection now,
Since Andy went a-droving.

Who now shall wear the cheerful face
In times when things are slackest?
And who shall whistle round the place
When Fortune frowns her blackest?

Oh, who shall cheek the squatter now
When he comes round us snarling?
His tongue is growing hotter now
Since Andy crossed the Darling.

Oh, may the showers in torrents fall,
And all the tanks run over;
And may the grass grow green and tall
In pathways of the drover;

And may good angels send the rain
On desert stretches sandy;
And when summer comes again
God grant 'twill bring us Andy.

Queen Of The Earth

An opal known as Queen of the Earth was found by Jack Dunstan, a gouger at Lightning Ridge. New South Wales, and sold by him for £100. It was later bought by the American tycoon, John Rockefeller, who paid £750.000 for it.

Boozing

'Drunkenness, it is well known, has ever been the prevailing vice of New South Wales and the fruitful source of more than half of the crimes committed in it.'

Governor Gipps, Sydney 1844

Celebrities

'Sydney is the Mecca of the decrepit author The last one they saw was Robert Louis Stevenson . . . When I arrived with nothing more than a brass band and a steam roller to herald my coming, I was received with the most gratifying enthusiasm.'

Somerset Maughan 1921

The rush to win exploring honours is depicted in this cartoon showing a race between John O'Hara Burke (on camel) and the central Australian explorer John McDouall Stuart

In Memoriam

The tragedy of the ill-fated expedition of Robert O'Hara Burke led to a wave of sentiment throughout Australia. Burke with the scientist, William John Wills, led an expedition from Melbourne through the interior to the Gulf of Carpenteria in 1860-61 The death of Burke, Wills and Charles Gray and the discovery of the bodies of Burke and Wills by a rescue expedition added to the hysteria that surrounded the huge memorial service that was held for them in Melboume and the erection of a memorial statue to them

The explorers Burke and Wills struggled back from the Gulf of Carpentaria only to find their base camp at Coopers Creek deserted with only a small cache of food left for them. The subsequent death of Burke and Wills is the most tragic story of Australian exploration

John Norton's Pen

Controversial Sydney newspaper proprietor, John Norton, had a most vitriolic pen, which he wielded indiscriminately in his own paper Truth in the late 1 9th century. Some samples:

On deeming the murder. . . The dastard demoniac, dubbed Deeming, deserves the doom of a degrading dog's death for diabolical deeds, if demonstrated without doubt that he is the doer.

On Prince Alfred, Duke of Edinburgh . . . one of the most prurient-minded, lecherous-living, brothel-bilking, tradesmen-tricking rascals that ever run amok.

He left this colony amid the howls of the harlots whom he bilked and the lamentations of the poor washerwomen whom he had refused to pay for the disagreeable task of washing his doubly dirty linen. Traced and tracked to New Zealand, he was, under threats of detention and legal process, compelled to pay for his dirty living and settle some of his tradesmen's bills.

Queen Victoria . . . Her chief claim to the remembrance of posterity will be that she has been the means of afflicting the English people with a most prolific brood of pestiferous German pauper pensioners, who comprise some of the most physically and morally scabby specimens of the human genus extant . . .

Caroline Chisholm

"Australia has up to now but one saint, one legend. This saint is an Englishwoman '. So wrote the French historian, Michelet of Caroline Chisholm, who earned the respect of the colony through her tireless work on behalf of the poor, the homeless and the underprivileged. Amongst her many achievements were the establishment of schools for girls, an 'immigrant's' home for unemployed women, work for the improvement of conditions on immigrant ships, the sponsoring of large groups of women for employment in country areas, and obtaining free passages for the wives and families of convicts who had been transported earlier.

A CAROL ON CAROLINE CHISHOLM

Beyond the roaring ocean, beneath the soil we tread
You've Englishmen and women well housed and clothed and fed
Who but for health and guidance to leave our crowded shores
Would now be stealing. begging, or starving at our doors.
Who taught them self-reliance and stirred them to combine
And club their means together to get across the brine?
Who led their expeditions and under whose command
Through dangers and through hardships sought they the promised land?
A second Moses, surely, it was who did it all
It was a second Moses in a bonnet and a shawl.
By means of one good lady were all these wonders wrought
By Caroline Chisholm's energy, benevolence and thought

The Little Digger

William Morris Hughes, the stormy petrel of Australian politics, was born in 1862 in London of Welsh parents. Aftermigrating to the colonies in 1884, he worked his way around the continent as a railway ganger, station hand and sea cook. Later he became a shopkeeper in the Sydney suburb of Balmain and became active in the Australian Workers' Union. At the turn of the century he formed the Waterside Workers' Federation.

At the first federal election 1901 he was voted Member for West Sydney in the House of Representatives and in 1915 he became Prime Minister. In the following year he attempted to introduce conscription in defiance of Labor Party policy. Faced with a walkout by his ministers he formed the National Party. As Prime Minister he visited Australian troops fighting in Europe who dubbed him "The Little Digger '. He enraged the British High Command by refusing to introduce the death penalty for AIF troops charged with desertion and further embarrassed Britain by demanding the right to sing the Peace as a separate, independent nation.

He made a triumphant return to Australia reflected in these words from a popular song of the day:

"And at all official ftmctions and other great shiroos,
They gave King George a seat beside our little Billy Hughes".

Hughes lost the Prime Ministership in 1923 but remained a member of the House or Representatives until his death in 1952. Labor never forgave him for splitting the Party and joining the opposition and when harangued in the House by Labor politicians he developed the habit of switching off his hearing aid.

During the Great War two colleagues threatened his uneasy coalition, Watt, a Victorian member and John Forrest the redoubtable West Australian explorer "They fought like Kilkenny cats," he recalled. He hit upon a unique solution by having Forrest created a peer of the realm and sending him to the British House of Lords. The Palace was horrified but Hughes had his way and found that "everything in the garden was lovely. I would have made him a bloody duke if necessary."

To the end he remained the despair of his secretaries discarding prepared speeches (copies of which had already been distributed to the press) to speak off the cuff on completely different topics. He insisted on driving himself from Sydney to Canberra and became a national safety hazard. clinging to the steering wheel "like a monkey on a stick" as Morris West one of his many secretaries recalled, and often driving on the wrong side of the road.

Governor Lachlan Macqauarie

The Building Governor

Lachlan Macquarie was one of the best loved of the Colonial Governors. A dour Scot he ushered in a new period of law and order after the infamous 'Rum Rebellion' when at the comand of his regiment, the 73rd Highlanders, he took the reigns of power from the New South Wales Corps and sent the Corps officers back to England.

As Govemor, Macquarie had an unprecedented twelve year term of office and during his term he fought to redress the social divisions in the colonial community. He encouraged emancipated convicts to take worthwhile positions in the community. elevating one, Francis Greenway to the position of Colonial Architect Under Macquarie's patronage Greenway built many of the fine buildings, churches, courthouses and schools which caused Macquarie to be dubbed "the building governor ' by his detractors, generally the free settlers who had lost their power under his firm rule.

Macquarie also encouraged exploration notably the endeavour of Blaxland, Wentworth and Lawson who discovered the way over the Blue Mountains. Macquarie put an end to the rum trade, introduced New South Wales' first coinage and established the Bank of New South Wales. This lavish expenditure combined with complaints from his critics caused the home government to appoint Commissioner Bigge to investigate his rule.

The building governor sailed from Sydney in February 1822, preparing to face his critics with this report

"I found the colony barely emerging from infantile imbecility, and suffering from various privations and disabilities; the country impenetrable beyond forty miles from Sydney; agriculture in a yet languishing state; commerce in its early dawn, revenue unknown; threatened with famine; distracted by faction; the public buildings in a state of dilapidation and mouldering to decay; the few roads and bridges formerly constructed rendered almost impassable; the population in general depressed by poverty; no public credit nor private confidence; the morals of the great mass of the population in the lowest state of debasement and religious worship almost totally neglected

Such was the state of New South Wales when I took charge of its administration on the 1st of January 1810 I left it in February last reaping incalculable advantages from my important and extensive discoveries in all directions, including the supposed insurmountable barrier called the Blue Mountains to the westward of which are situated the fertile plains of Bathurst and, in all respects, enjoying a state of private comfort and public prosperity which I trust will at least equal the expectation of His Majesty's Government

That the Colony has, under my orders and regulations, greatly improved in agriculture, trade, increase of flocks and herds, and wealth of every kind; that the people build better dwelling houses, and live more comfortably; that they are in a very considerable degree refomred in their moral and religious hablts that they are now less prone to drunkeness, and more industrious; and that crimes have decreased, making due allowance for the late great increase of convict population; every candid liberal minded man, at all acquainted with the history of the colony for the last twelve years, will readily attest

Macquarie, broken in spirit and health, was denied recognition by a thankless Homc government but within a year of his departure his admirers in Sydney were singing

The Old Viceroy
Macquarie was the prince of men!
Australia's pride and joy!
We never shall see his like again
Bring back the Old Viceroy!

When news of his death reached Sydney Town in 1824 church bells toiled, families shuttered their windows, the Sydney Gazette announced his passing in borders of black and a poet echoed the Colony's grief

'Weep, Nation, Weep!
Macquarie is no more

Australian Humour

Humour

The Australian of the bush or the outback of earlier days, the working man and men in the Armed Forces are noted for a particular brand of humour delivered in a flat laconic style, with the most fantastic exaggeration made credible by the dead-pan delivery. Often the twist in the tale to the listener is the realisation that he is being had. Our forbears, the convicts, migrants and settlers. bullock drivers, shearers, miners, swagmen and itinerant labourers, lived a hard battling life, and from this sprang not only the camaraderie of the Australian working man but also the rough deprecating sardonic humour that is ever present in the jokes and stories that that have been handed down. A sample of the great Australian joke is told by C. E. W. Bean in his book The Dreadnought of the Darling published in London in 1911:

Two mates had been carrying their swags in company for some time along the interminable road that leads always to the horizon.

Early one morning up a creek bed to the side of them they passed a big black object which, whatever it was, had clearly been dead for some days. About midday Bill took his pipe out of his mouth. "D'yer see that dead ox?" he grunted. The shadows of the evening were closing around them when Jim spat solemnly into the camp fire. "'Twasn't an ox, 'twas a horse," he said. After that he turned in and slept eight well deserved hours. When he awoke there was no sign of Bill or Bill's swag. Bill was clearly gone. Only a grimy note was left stuck in a cleft stick. "There's too much argyment in this 'ere camp," it said.

'ORACE: *"When do yer know when you've had enough?"*
CUTHBERT - *"Next morning."*
Cecil Hartt SMITH'S WEEKLEY 1929

Here is a sample of other Australian jokes of earlier times:

James "Hungry" Tyson was a squatter who was famous for his meanness. When he visited one of his properties in New South Wales all the children were dressed up in their best clothes. The wife of one of the station hands said to him, "There's a fine lot, Mr. Tyson." "Yes," said Tyson bleakly, "but they don't grow any wool."

On a Queensland station the squatter had one of his Aboriginal stockmen peddling furiously on the peddle radio so that he could listen to reports of the test cricket in England. The weary stockman was kept at it hard into the night as Don Bradman piled up a great score of runs. Finally the stockman exclaimed, "Crikey. this Bradman must be good. How many could he make in the daylight."

Two shearers were true to the competitive spirit of the shearing shed. Apart from trying to get the best tally for the day they competed with each other for speed in everything that they did. They were washing their shirts one Sunday afternoon and Joe claimed that he had finished first. Fred disagreed and an argument developed. At last Fred said in disgust, "All right throw the bloody thing in the dirt and I'll give you another go."

Some shearers were talking about the sheds they had worked in. An old shearer topped the lot. "The biggest shed I ever worked in had 100 stands on each side," he said. "You could get the sack on one side, cross the boards and be hired on the other. "

The world got around that a young soldier had been a crack kangaroo shooter before the start of the war in 1914. A Sergeant told him that they were going to make him a sniper. He said he wouldn't do it "I've shot kangaroos, wallabies, rabbits. dingos and donkeys and I ain't going to finish up with men—at least not by sniping at them anyhow." The Sergeant bullied him but he remained adament. "Killing a kangaroo is different from killing a man," he said. "Alright," said the Sergeant, "if you are that finicky I'll go over and ask Fritz to hop."

BUSH VOCABULARY

HORSEMAN:
"See a cow with a calf 'long the road old man?"

OLD MAN:
"No; but I see a bloke with a calf a bit back"

HORSEMAN:
"He's the cow I'm after"

An old stockman was threatened with the sack because he kept turning up late for work. After it happened repeatedly the boss put him on his last chance. but the next day he was late again. The boss walked up to him, "Right, that is it Bill. You are late again." Old Bill replied, "Sorry boss but I just couldn't wake my flaming dogs."

Rain began to fall in a drought stricken part of the country and the farmer's son who had seen very little rain in his life-time, ran outside and danced about in the wet "Come in out of the rain you fool," shouted his father. "But I'm not getting wet, Dad", his son protested. "I'm not worried about you," shouted the farmer, "but you are keeping the rain off the ground."

JACKEROO *"Curious effect the bush air has on certain parts of the body, don't y' know."*
BUSHIE: *"As how?"*
JACKEROO: *"Well. you've lived here all your life, and I've only just come out; look at me I nearly bounce out of the saddle when I hit it, and you don't bounce at all, don't y know."*

Frank Mahoney LONE HAND I908

A farmer met another with a broken down looking horse on a country road, and the following coversation took place.

FIRST FARMER, *"Morning."*
SECOND FARMER, *"Morning."*
FIRST FARMER, *"What did you dose that mare of yours with when she had the gripes?"*
SECOND FARMER, *"kerosene."*

Two days later the first farmer with no horse met the second farmer on a road.

FIRST FARMER, *"That horse of mine died when I gave him the kerosene."*
SECOND FARMER, *"So did mine."*
FIRST FARMER, *"Morning "*
SECOND FARMER, *"Morning. "*

"That was a narrow escape, miss; do you feel O.K ?"
"Heavenly; will you be on duty next Sunday?"
George Little AUSSIE 1924

A commercial traveller was doing his rounds in the far west He stopped at a cafe and found that their lunch consisted of the same thing he'd had for several days, corned mutton and potatoes. He said to the young girl serving him, "Do you have any pickles please?" "Hang on," she said and walked to the kitchen door, and called out "Hey, Mum, there's a silly coot here who thinks it's Christmas."

A publican's wife poured a very ungenerous mixture of whisky to an old bushman who had come in for a night on the town. The bushman eyed it somberly. "What's the matter?" said the barmaid. "I'll have you know that whisky is 30 years old." "Well then," said the bushman, "it's very small for its age."

At a station where an Aboriginal stockman worked, flood waters marooned the main herd of cows on a strip of high ground. The only way to save the cattle was to carry food to them across the swirling flood waters. The station boss said to the hand, "What about taking over a boat load of hay to the cows?" The Aboriginal stockman considered the matter and replied. "You'd better send a white man boss—they're still plentiful but fellows like me are getting too bloody scarce."

A boasting bushman got a job on a station and he told the boss what a great rider he was. When the boss called for a spirited horse that took some handling, the new hand jumped on the horse and when it began to skitter he flogged it till it wouldn't move. The boss came back to see the end of the flogging incident. ' Well said the bushman, "I handled him all right boss. how am I going?" "On the first train out of town," said the boss bleakly.

One night in an outback pub a stranger began to skite about his droving exploits. After a while he turned to a hard bitten old character. "And what's the longest droving trip you've been on?" he asked patronisingly. Old Gob looked him squarely in the eye, "From Cape York to Hobart, son — and we walked them all the way."

One of the greatest struggles for the peppery Australian prime minister W M. Hughes was the conscription issue Hughes stumped the country advocating conscription but a referendum brought a 'no" vote.

Prime Minister, Billy Hughes, was a brilliant debater and never missed an opportunity to score on an opponent in the House. As a Labor Member he was making a ferocious attack on the policies of the then Attorney- General, Alfred Deakin and one statement brought Deakin to his feet, crying: "I deny it, I deny it." There was a dead silence in the House and Hughes stood in his place with his hand to his ear. Finally the Attorney General asked Hughes if he had finished his remarks and he replies: "Oh no, MR Speaker, I was just waiting for the cock to crow."

Mountain Of Rabbits

The great American writer, Mark Twain in his book “Following the Equator” tells the following tale. "The growing day and the early sun exposed the distant range called the Blue Mountains . . . A resident told me that these were not mountains: he said they were rabbit piles and explained that long exposure and the overripe condition of the rabbits was what made them look so blue. This man may have been right, but much reading of books of travel has made me distrustful of gratis information furnished by official residents of a country. The facts which such people give to travellers are usually erroneous, and often intemperately so. The rabbit plague has indeed been very bad in Australia and it could account for one mountain but not for a mountain range, it seems to me. It is too large an order."

The Austra-laise

C. J. Dennis produced a poem for Australia entitled A Real Australian Austra-laise which he submitted to the National Song Competition organised by the Bulletin in 1908. It was awarded a special prize of one guinea, and the judges said, " It will win its way to every heart in the backblocks."

Dennis revised it for the Australian Expeditionary forces in 1916, for singing to the tune of Onward Christian Soldiers It begins:

Fellers of Australia
Blokes an' coves an coots,
Shift yer - carcasses,
Move yer - boots,
Gird yer - loins up,
Get yer - gun,
Set the - enemy
An' watch the blighters run.

Chorus:
Geta - move on,
Have some - sense,
Learn the - art of
Self de - fence

A MONOPOLIST

"You're a greatbloke ferthe wimmen, Josko; but are yer sure yer love Lisa alone?" "My oath; I'd rather love 'er alone than with a crowd any day."

Adam Plass THE GADFLY 1907

THE HUMOUR OF THE CLERGY

MRS MALONEY: *"Is it going ye are, yer riverince? Sure an' ye haven't seen my last baby."*
FATHER CASSIDY: *"No. Mrs Maloney; an' I niver expect to!"*

Livingstone Hopkins THE BULLETIN c. 1890

Celebrities

Anthony Trollope was possibly the most famous novelist to visit Australasia in the late 19th century and his account of his travels during 1871 and 1872 contain some telling observations of the local scene.

One trait he observed was our habit of bragging. He also, incorrectly, predicted that Australian independence would become inevitable when 'the leading men...have been born in Australia, so as to have grown up without the still existing feeling that England is their inevitable home'.

D. H. Lawrence, arriving at Thirroul a small town south of Sydney, in May 1922, gloried in the anonymity. 'We don't know a soul,' he wrote. 'For the first time in my life I feel how lovely it is to know nobody.'

In June and July, before leaving for Mexico, Lawrence wrote Kangaroo, in which his character spoke of 'the vast uninhabited land...so hoary and lost, so unapproachable'; and of 'these British Australians with their aggressive familiarity!'

Parliamentary Humour

Fred Daly, a member of Australia's Parliament for 32 continuous years was one of its liveliest wits. As a member and Cabinet Minister who served under ten Prime Ministers and rubbed shoulders with all the major political figures of three decades, Fred Daly was a wonderful raconteur and he collected a store of Parliamentary wit a lot of which he produced in his autobiography "From Curtin to Kerr." Here are some samples.

A well- known politician once walked around a crowded room, shook hands with everybody and asked an old acquaintance how his father was and was advised that he had died some time ago. The politician kept going around shaking hands and when he came to his acquaintance again asked, "How is your father?" He received the reply, "Still dead."

A typical example of Billy Hughes' fighting wit came with his statement in the House, "The Honourable Member is not fit to swill milk to pigs." When the Member objected Billy said, "Very well, the Honourable Member is fit to swill milk to pigs."

The Treasurer in the Menzies Government Arthur Fadden, was sharp witted and a very effective speaker, particularly on the public platform, but this time he had a joke turned against him. He said to an interjector, "Look my friend, I work when you are asleep " To which the interjector replied, "Of course you do. You are a bloody burglar."

At another meeting Fadden said in desperation to a constant interjector, "Look my friend, when I was a boy I ill-treated a donkey and my mother said, 'Arty, that donkey will come back and haunt you'. She was right" said Fadden, "you have turned up tonight."

The biting humour of the tough Labor member for East Sydney, Eddy Ward, is illustrated in this story about Bert Lazzarini, who was Assistant Treasurer in the Curtin Government Lazzarini was a real old- time Labor member who used to wear a sweater with pockets in which he constantly put his hands, thus lengthening the sweater until it was almost down to his knees. One day Eddy Ward announced that Lazzarini was in hospital for an operation. "What for?" he was asked. "To have his sweater removed" said Ward.

Arthur Fadden scored a few points off his Prime Minister, Sir Robert Menzies. When they were walking together at John Curtin's funeral Menzies remarked, "I don't want all this fuss when I go, Arty. " " Don't worry, " replied Fadden "you won't get it"

Menzies had a lot of run-ins with the fiery Speaker of the House, Sir Archy Cameron. He once said to him, "Archy, I do not suffer fools gladly." Cameron replied, "It might be news to you to know that ruddy fools have a lot of trouble putting up with you too."

Cameron once told Eddy Ward to "bow low and apologise". Ward bowed to the Speaker's chair but Cameron said, "You have not bowed low enough." "How low do you want me to bow?" asked Ward. Cameron replied, "How low can you get?"

Gough Whitlam was a prime target of Eddy Ward's animosity. Once Ward did his block and chased Whitlam down the corridor and swung a punch at him. He missed and lost his spectacles. Whitlam disappeared into a room and Ward like a blind man was on all fours on the floor groping around for his spectacles. Some time later during a period of ill health Ward was asked when had he first realised his health was slipping. He replied "The day that I missed Whitlam."

Arthur Calwell had his great moments as a humorous speaker. On one occasion in Sydney, Ward, Evatt Calwell and Daly spoke to about 10,000 people during a Referendum

Campaign. Calwell was in top form. "Last night in Albury," he said "a man told me he would not trust anybody with these powers. I asked him if he would trust me with them and he said he did not know. I said, what about Eddy Ward? 'I have my doubts about that,' was the reply. I then asked if he would trust Dr. Evatt 'By jove, you are stretching it a bit now,' he said." The only one who laughed was Calwell. Ward and Evatt sat grim and silent while the crowd roared with laughter

Fred Daly had many verbal tussles with Jim Killen on the other side. Daly reports, "After what I considered one of my reasonably good speeches, Killen followed and said that the speech of the Minister, Mr. Daly, reminded him of the Irishman in the dock. The judge said 'How do you plead?' 'I don't know,' said the Irishman. 'I haven't heard the evidence yet' "

Extracted with permission of the author from *From Curtin to Kerr.* by Fred Daly, published by Sun Books Pty. Ltd.

CONSOLING VERY NERVOUS PASSENGER:
'Oh, Mr Sailor, do you think there is any fear of us drowning?"
SEAMAN: *"Oh. no, mum; not the least Why, this place is full of sharks."*
Pat Sullivan THE GADELY I907.

The Menzies Touch

Sir Robert Menzies had a touch with interjectors that has not been surpassed by any Australian politician. Some examples.

WOMAN INTERJECTOR: *"I wouldn't vote for you if you were the Archangel Gabriel."* **MENZIES:** *"If I were the Archangel Gariel madam, I am afraid you wouldn't be in my electorate."*

HECKLER: *"Wot you ganna do about 'ousing?"*

MENZIES: *"Put an H in front of it.*

MENZIES TO AN INTERJECTOR AT A MELBOURNE UNIVERSITY MEETING: *No Government has ever promoted education as I have. After listening to you I can understand what vast amounts will still have to be spent."*

Humour In Court

The following examples of humour in court and the legal profession are taken from The Lawyer Who Laughed by A. S. Gillespie Jones (Hutchinson).

In the Court of Petty Sessions at Carlton, a man was charged with using offensive and obscene language in a public place. A dear old lady gave the evidence and handed up the offending words on a piece of paper. The Magistrate glanced at them and handed the piece of paper down to the defendant, who denied using the words. The defendant went into the witness box and gave evidence on oath.

He said, "I am a linesman, Your Worship, and I was working down the bottom of a telegraph pole. My mate, Harry, was soldering on a ladder at the top of the pole and he dropped some boiling hot solder and it went down the back of my neck and was caught between my shirt and my bare skin. All I said was: 'Harry, in future, you really must be more careful'."

DEFENCE COUNSEL: "And I suggest to you, witness, that you suggested to my client's wife, that you and she commit adultery, over the telephone?"

OPPOSING COUNSEL: "In that case, Your Honour, and if it be proved, then I suggest that my client has his 'phone cut off!"

The black maria arrived at Long Bay Penitentiary and a lone figure was hustled out of the back of the van into the sergeant's office. The sergeant said to the prisoner, "What are you in for?"

The prisoner replied, "I got seven years for forgery."

The sergeant said, "Empty out your pockets; I have to enter these upon a property sheet."

The man emptied out his pockets and the sergeant laboriously wrote out the items. At the end, he said to his prisoner, "Read these over and see if they are correct."

The man said, "I can't read."

The sergeant said, "Don't give me that you just got seven years for forgery. Don't muck about, read it and sign it."

The man repeated, "I can't read."

The sergeant said, "All right, all right, all right I'll humour you, I'll read it and you check the items." The sergeant read it out and said, "Is that right?"

The man said, "Yes."

The sergeant said, "Sign it"

The man said, "I can't write. '

The sergeant said, "Look, of course you can write, you just got seven years for forgery. Now sign your name."

The man repeated, "I can't write."

The sergeant said, "Of course you can write, how did you get seven years for forgery, if you can't write?"

The prisoner pondered for a moment and said, "Well, I think I must have had a bad lawyer."

The late Chief Justice, Sir John Latham, had certain troubles with the traffic laws when he was a member of the Commonwealth Parliament and before he became Chief Justice of the High Court of Australia.

He was driving in St Kilda Road, Melbourne, when he offended against a traffic law. A young Irish constable stopped him and said, "What would be your name?"

Sir John said "John Latham."

The constable said, "You wouldn't be after being that same John Latham who is a barrister, now would you?"

Sir John said, "Yes, I am that same man."

"And you wouldn't be after being that same John Latham who is a King's Counsel, now would you?"

Sir John said, "Yes, I am that same man."

"And you wouldn't be after being that same John Latham who is the Commonwealth Attorney-General?"

Sir John, whose hopes had begun to rise, said, "Yes, I am he."

The constable then said, "Well, you won't be able to plead ignorance of the Law, now will you?"

DOCTOR: *"Your husband must have absolute rest, madam."*
MRS STAMP: *"Well, he's due back at the office on Monday."*
J. C. Bancke TABTE TATK 1928

Country juries are wonderful and they know more about their neighbours than judges, barristers and policemen give them credit for.

The classic story of a jury was at Dubbo, where a jury tried a man on a charge of stealing some heifers. When the jury returned with their verdict, the Associate said, "Do you find the accused guilty or not guilty of cattle-stealing?" To which the foreman replied, "Not guilty, if he returns the cows."

The Judge read the jury the Riot Act and he concluded by saying, "Go out and reconsider your verdict. You swore that you would try the issue between our Sovereign Lady, the Queen, and the prisoner and find a true verdict according to the evidence."

The jury retired again and when they returned some hour and a half later, they had a most belligerent air about them. The Associate said, "Have you decided on your verdict?" The foreman said, "Yes, we have. We find the accused not guilty—and he doesn't have to return the cows."

'Pig Iron Bob'

Menzies' announcement of his decision to continue to supply Japan with pig iron from Australian foundries before the war earned for him the ignominious nickname 'Pig Iron Bob' and prompted the following, sung to the tune of 'There'll Always Be An England', mocking two giants, one industrial and one political:

"There'll always be a Menzies
While there's a B.H.P.
He's selling off their scrap iron
— And it's on the A.B.C.!"

Hop Cartoon Bedfellows — but sleepily with on eye open Bulletin, 21 Feb 1891.

Pioneer Pannikins

Australians have earned a reputation for their dry and laconic wit Long, droll stories with the most unexpected punch lines were often told by men on the land. Charles Macalistcr recounted such a story in "Old Pioneering Days in the Steamy South".

One day in the summer of 1847, Mr. Murray and the author were returning homewards from Goulburn, and at the old crossing place over the Wondinilly, at Kenmore, we met the late Francis McArthur, then owner of Norwood. Mr. McArthur, as old hands will remember, was of a very genial disposition, and as we had some spirits with us, we asked "Black Francis," as McArthur was called, to have a 'nip'. But neither of us at that moment could find a pannikin handy. Mr. Murray, however, taking the author's bullock-bell, rinsed it in the river and handing it to Mr. McArthur he said, "We've lost the run on the pannikins; but never mind, here's the bullock-bell—try a drop out of that."

"Well," said McArthur, "that's a better tumbler than the one I had the other day. I was out on the plains with one of my men looking for horses, and we had a bottle of rum with us, but no tumbler or pannikin. But there was a blackfellow's skull handy—so we drank out of that. Here's luck," he said, "and I hope when you want a drink, if you cannot find a blackfellow's skull, you'll never go short of a bullock-bell."

The Bush Wanderers

Whip, horse and dog are the tools of trade of the outback drover as he pushed cattle hundreds of miles across the dry and hostile inland plains

Where The Dead Men Lie

One of Australia's most promising poets; Barcroft Boake hanged himself with a stock whip at Sydney at the age of 26. Boake had been a drover in Queensland for several years and some of his poems carry a melancholic strain. His best known poem Where the Dead Men Lie opens:

Out on the wastes of the Never Never
That's where the dead men lie!
There where the head waves dance forever
That's where the dead men lie!
That's where the Earth's loved sons are keeping
Endless tryst: not the west winds sweeping
Feverish opinions can wake their sleeping —
Out where the dead men lie!

A Damper As Heavy As Lead

The ubiquitous food of the track and the outback station was the damper, so called because it was made in the ashes that were used to "damp down" a fire overnight by covering the blaze with the ash and embers of a fringe of a fire. G. C. Mundy in Our Antipodes, (London 1855) described the damper. "At a filthy cabin where he halted for the night some of us tasted for the first time the Australian bush bread. A baked unleavened dough called damper—a damper sure enough to the stoutest appetite— whence its name I suppose for it is as heavy as lead. Its manufacture is as follows: a wheaten paste is made, kneaded for a short time, flattened out into a muffin shaped dough, about the size of the top of an ordinary band box, and an inch or two thick; a part of the hearth stone is cleared of the wood ashes, the dough is dropped upon it, and the hot ashes raked over it: if not made too thick, the damper comes out done to a turn in about half an hour."

A recipe for damper is: take one pound of flour, water and a pinch of salt. Mix into a stiff dough and knead for at least one hour, not continuously but the longer it is kneaded the better the damper. Press with the hands into a flat cake and cook it in at least a foot of hot ashes. The damper was so much a part of the swagman's life that at Christmas time he put threepences in it and ate it as his Christmas pudding.

Bushmen playing cards around a campfire

The Real Clancy

The Clancy of A. B. "Banjo" Paterson's famous poem Clancy of the Overflow is said to have been Thomas Gerald Clancy who came from Cork, Ireland, with his parents to Melbourne in 1841. A newspaper account of how Clancy drove a huge herd of cattle from the Overflow station was the inspiration for Paterson's poems. The Overflow was a station on the Lachlan River in New South Wales. Paterson and Clancy subsequently met in Sydney where the poet witnessed Clancy's will.

The Goulburn River.

CLANCY OF THE OVERFLOW

I had written him a letter which I had, for want of better
Knowledge, sent to where I met him down the Lachlan, years ago,
He was shearing when I knew him, so I sent the letter to him,
Just 'on spec', addressed as follows, 'Clancy, of The Overflow'.

And an answer came directed in a writing unexpected,
(And I think the same was written with a thumb-nail dipped in tar)
'Twas his shearing mate who wrote it, and verbatim I will quote it:
'Clancy's gone to Queensland droving, and we don't know where he are.'

In my wild erratic, fancy visions come to me of Clancy
Gone a-droving 'down the Cooper' where the Western drovers go;
As the stock are slowly stringing, Clancy rides behind them singing,
For the drover's life has pleasures that the townsfolk never know.

And the bush hath friends to meet him, and their kindly voices greet him
In the murmur of the breezes and the river on its bars,
And he sees the vision splendid of the sunlit plains extended,
And at night the wond'rous glory of the everlasting stars.

I am sitting in my dingy little office, where a stingy
Ray of sunlight struggles feebly down between the houses tall
And the foetid air and gritty of the dusty, dirty city
Through the open window floating, spreads its foulness over all.

And in place of lowing cattle, I can hear the fiendish rattle
Of the tramways and the 'buses making hurry down the street,
And the language uninviting of the gutter children fighting,
Comes fitfully and faintly through the ceaseless tramp of feet

And the hurrying people daunt me, and their pallid faces haunt me
As they shoulder one another in their rush and nervous haste,
With their eager eyes and greedy, and their stunted forms and weedy,
For townsfolk have no time to grow, they have no time to waste.

And I somehow rather fancy that I'd like to change with Clancy,
Like to take a turn at droving where the seasons come and go,
While he faced the round eternal of the cash-book and the journal —
But I doubt he'd suit the office, Clancy, of The Overflow.

BULLOCKY-OH!

Well, I draw for Speckle's Mill, bullocky-oh,
bullocky-oh And if s many the log I drew, bullocky-oh
I put cedar, beech and pine, and I never get on the wine,
I'm the king of bullock drivers, don't you know, bullocky-oh,
The king of bullock drivers, bullocky-oh.

There's Wapples, now, he brags, bullocky-oh,
bullocky-oh, Of his fourteen rawboned stage, bullocky-oh.
I can give him a thousand feet square and never cheat,
I'm the king of bullock drivers, don't you known, bullocky-oh,
I'm the king of bullock drivers, bullocky-oh.

There' s Luinea and Andleson, too, bullocky- oh,
bullocky- oh, If s many the leg they drew, bullocky-oh.
And I say it is no slander when I reckon I get their dander.
When they hear the crack of my whip, bullocky-oh, bullocky-oh,
When they hear the crack of my whip, bullocky-oh.

The bushmen of early Australia — the stockmen, drovers. bullock drivers and shearers— were the heroes of pioneering and became legendary for their toughness and resourcefulness. This picture is of a group of Queensland station hands in the mid-1900s.

BULLOCKY BILL

As I came down Talbingo Hill
I heard a maiden cry,
"There goes old Bill the Bullocky
He's bound for Gundagai."

A better poor old beggar
Never cracked an honest crust
A tougher poor old beggar
Never drug a whip through dust

His team got bogged on the Five-mile trek
Bill clashed and swore and cried
"If Nobbie don't get me out of this
I'll tattoo his bloddy hide."

But Nobbie strained and broke the yoke
And poked out the leader's eye,
Then the dog sat on the tucker-box
Five miles from Gundagai.

Bullock team carting red cedar.

Mateship

In the solitude of the bush, in the station yard or the shearing shed, in the turmoil of war, at work and at play Australian men built up an ethic of mateship that became a lasting characteristic. Henry Lawson penned this essay on mateship in 1911:

The grandest stories ever written were the stories of two men. That holds good up to our own times, from Sydney Carton and Charles Darnay to Tennessee's Partner and Tennessee

I can always see Sydney Carton mounting the scaffold to the guillotine, his hands tied behind, a dreamy far-away expression in his eyes; his hair bound back in its riband, much more carefully than was usual with him; himself clothed more tidily than was usual with him, because he was supposed to be the man for the sake of whose wife and little girl he was about to die. Poor Sydney was a drunkard, and perhaps that is why some of us are drawn to him all the more.

And Tennessee's Partner at the Court of Judge Lynch: "An' I answers you fair and square, Jedge, as between man and man, 'What should a man know about his partner?' " And Tennessee's Partner knew all:

And Tennessee's Partner, with his donkey Jenny and cart, and rough coffin, in the shadow of the trees, after the lynching. He didn't want to hurry the gentlemen at all. "But if yer quite done with Tennessee, my partner thar"' — And the last glimpse of Tennessee, the grave filled up—the grave in the little digger's vegetable garden (I've seen them in Australia)— Tennessee sitting on the foot of the mound, wiping his face with his red bandana handkerchief.

They used to say I was influenced by Bret Harte. I hope so. I read Tennessee's Partner and the other stories when I was about thirteen, and Dickens a little later on. Bret Harte died near to where I lived in England, by the way.

Tennessee forgave his partner the greatest wrong that one man can do another; and that's one thing that mateship can do.

The man who hasn't a male mate is a lonely man indeed, or a stranger man, though he has a wife and family. I believe that there are few such men. If the mate isn't here, he is somewhere else in the world, or perhaps he may be dead.

Marcus Clarke speaks of a recaptured convict being asked where his mate was, in a tone as if a mate were something a convict was born with—like a mole for instance. When I was on the track alone for a stretch, I was always asked where my mate was, or if I had a mate.

And so it is, from "Boko Bill" (bottle-oh!) and "Three-Pea Ginger" of Red Rock Lane, up or down — or up and down— to Percy and Harold who fraternise at the Union Club. Bill gets "pinched" for shifting cases from a cart, or something of that sort, and Ginger who is "pretty swift with the three-pea", but never rises above a little safe "thieving" or paltry swindling, and is, therefore, never likely to need serious "outside" assistance, works for Bill for all he is worth, in fact But in spite of the positive and unanimous testimony of "Frowsy Sal" (one time "The Red Streak"), Bill s piece ', "Ginger", "The Red Rover", "One-eyed Kate", "Stousher", "Pincher" and as many other equally respectable and well-known ladies and gentlemen as the court will listen to, Bill goes up for a "sixer".

Ginger's work doesn't end here. Others are "pinched" and sent up, and they take messages in to Bill, and arrange with certain prisoners who are "on tobacco" to help Bill, and be helped themselves when they come out Poor Pincher being pinched, Sal says to him: "If you do get fixed, Pincher, tell Bill I'm stickin'."

Presently the word goes round that Frowsy Sal is stickin' ter Boko Bill and is receivied, for the most part, with blasphemous incredulity by the "talent". But Sal cooks in third-rate public-houses, and washes and works hard to keep the kid, the room, and the "sticks", and have a few shillings for Bill again when he comes out, and she keeps "the blokes" out of her kitchen. Which facts are commented on with yet further wondering blasphemy, into which creeps a note almost of reverence.

So Ginger, being Bill's cobber, is deputed to send round the hat to help Sal, because Sal is sticking to Bill. It is a furtive hat, but the money comes in, and so Ginger sticks to Bill through Sal. The money is from thievish hearts and thievish hands but the hearts o' men are there all the same.

Hearts o' men are kind to Sal in other places. The warder inside the jail lays a kindly hand on her shoulder, and says. Come along my girl" But Sal has no use for sympathy, and little for kindness. "Blarst their eyes!" she says. "They can always ketch and jail better men than themselves. If it wasn't for the likes of poor Bill they'd have to go to work themselves, from the Guvnor, blarst 'em!"

Let's have a look where Bill is, and though I might seem to be on the branch tracks from my subject the red thread is running all through.

If you go in "under the Government", and not as a visitor, you might be the Duke of All-That- Is, and yet little Cooney, who is finishing a sentence for breakin' 'n' enterin', and is "on tobacco", is a greater man than you. Because he is on tobacco which is worth twice its weight in gold in jail, and can lend bits to his mates.

In jail the initiated help the awkward newcomers all they can. There is much sympathy and practical human kindness cramped and cooped up in jail. A goodconduct prisoner with a "billet" — say, warder or pantry-man in the hospital or observation ward or cook or assistant in some position which enables him to move about—will often risk his billet food and comfort (aye, and extra punishment) in order to smuggle tobacco to a prisoner whom he never met outside, and is never likely to meet again. And this is often done at the insistance of the prisoner's mate. Mateship again!

True mateship looks for no limelight. They say that self-preservation is the strongest instinct of mankind, it may come with the last gasp, but I think the preservation of the life or liberty of a mate — man or woman — is the first and strongest. It is the instinct that irresistibly impels a thirsty, parched man, out on the burning sands, to pour the last drop of water down the throat of a dying mate, where none save the sun or moon or stars may see. And the sun, moon and stars do not write to the newspapers. To give a weaker "partner"' the last sup of coffee, or bite of boiled beans and bacon, on the snow wastes of Alaska, where the rim of the sun only touches the rim of the south at noon. To give up the only place in the boats at sea, and die that perhaps most dreaded of all deaths — the death by drowning in mid-ocean.

And the simple heroes of common life! They come down to us from a certain Samaritan who journeyed down to Jericho one time, and pass — mostly through Dickens in my case. Kit Nubbles, the uncouth champion of Little Nell! The world is full of Kits, and this is one of the reasons why the world lasts. Young John Chivery, turnkey at the Marshalsea, who lived Little Dorrit! There was never a gentleman in all his family, he said; but he stood, in the end, the greatest gentleman in that book. All the others had something to gain— either money, fame, or a woman's love; but he had nothing. Mark Tapley, poor Tom Pinch, and simple Joe Gargery. Newman Noggs, the drink-ruined scarecrow and money-lender's drudge, wiping Little Kate Nickleby's eye with something that might have been his handkerchief, but looked like a duster, and risking his very bread to fight for her afterwards. Newman was a gentleman once, they said, and kept his dogs. I think he was a gentleman yet And little Snagsby, the mild and the hopelessly henpecked, with his little cough of deference behind his hand, and his furtive half-crown for a case of distress.

The creed of mateship embraces an old mate's wife, sons and daughters. "Yes, I'll lend you the money, Jack; don't mention it— your father an' me was mates on the diggings long before you was thought of, my boy." Or simply "I'm an old mate of your father's."

Mateship extends to an old absent mate's new mates and friends; as with the present generation of bush mates: "Why!" — with a surprise and joyful oath, and a mighty clout on the back or shoulder—"did you know Bill? Comeanavadrink!" And when you get confidential: "You don't happen to be stiff, do you? Don't be frightened to say so! There's always a quid or two there for any of blanky old Bill's friends as is hard up!" (Bill is still young, by the way.) And the mighty burst of joyous profanity when two bush mates meet after a separation of some years!

Visiting an old mate in the hospital! The broad grins! Bill wasn't used to being fixed up like that in the old days, with pretty nurses, in caps and uniforms, gliding round him. But there was a woman —

Bill-o'-th'bush being dead, Jim and Mates bury him, and Jim blubbers and is unashamed. Later it is Jim's sad duty to take round the hat and gather in the quids for poor Bill's missus and kids. And Jim sticks to them, and helps them all he can; though Bill's missus always hated

Jim like poison, and Jim "could never stand her".

In ordinary cases, when a man or woman is in a hole—and the man need not be a saint. nor the woman any better than she ought to be, either—the hat is started round with bad swear words of unnecessary vehemence, lest some —— might cherish a suspicion that there is any sentiment behind it all. "Chuck in half a quid and give the poor —— a show!"

Another kind of case — a little story of two men who went up and down in the world. One mate went up because Fortune took a fancy to him, and he didn't discredit Fortune; the other went down because he drank, and Luck forbade to camp by his fire. In later years the pair came together, and the mate who was up gave the mate who was down a billet in his business in town, and bore with him with boundless patience, and took him back time and again. And it came to pass that one day the mate who was down saved the life of the little girl of the mate who was up. Forthwith the mate who was down rolled up his swag and took the track, without even giving the mate who was up a chance to thank him. He felt he couldn't meet him and look him in the face again. And the old mate who was up understood. It was an extremely awkward and embarrassing case all round. A monetary gift was absolutely impossible — utterly out of the question; and it was equally impossible for them to continue comfortably in their old relations. The only way to mend matters would have been for the mate who was up to save the life of the child of the mate who was down, in return; but the mate who was down, didn't have a child that he knew of. He went away, and straightened up, and did not return until he was on his feet and the late affair had had time to blow over.

A man will more often reform because of a good or heroic deed he has done, and has not been rewarded for, than a foolish or bad one he has done and been punished for. Punishment does not reform men.

Mateship is jealous at times; and, if any jealousy can be unselfish, free from vindictiveness, and even noble, this can be. Which reminds me of an incident in the mateship of Bob Lucas and Jim Barnes, professional shearers, west of the Darling River.

Bob was a good cove, a straight chap, a white man. So was Jim, so long as he kept away from drink, cards, dice, and headin' 'em. They had lost sight of each other for two or three years, and it had been whispered that Bob had been in trouble, but for "nothin' bad". But it wasn't whispered in Jim's presence, for he was always overeager to fight where Bob's name was concerned.

But there came a man, or a chap, to the shed where Bob and Jim shore—or rather, a cove, in the vague sense of the term. Some of the chaps referred to him as "a——". Call him Cooney. Cooney was short and stout or rather fat, where some men would be burly, or nuggety. He had, where it showed through holes in his rags, the unhealthy pallid fatness of the tramp or jail-bird who hasn't worked for a long time. He had no moustache, but stubble nearly all over his face. He had no proper swag, just a roll of rags on a string he had no water-bag, only a billy. To the surprise of some, Bob recognized him and went and spoke to him. And Bob gave him tobacco, and spoke to the boss over the board, and got him on picking-up in the place of a rouse-about who was leaving.

Jim was greatly disgusted, for Cooney was picking-up for him and Bob and three others, and was no good. "We'll cut out in a week or so, and he'll get into it," said Bob. "Give the man a show " Jim and mates grumbled, but mateship forbode to ask Bob's reasons for sticking to the——. It was the etiquette of mateship. But Cooney, who was short of something in his head, got worse, instead of better, though Bob helped him all he could, and Cooney had to be put off when an old hand turned up. But Bob stuck to him, got him a few things from the store, and arranged about his tucker for a day or two.

Cooney seemed neither slouching nor sullen, but he kept vaguely and unobtrusively to himself. He would sit smoking in the row by the hut after tea. His manner suggested that of a mild, harmless, deaf man of rather low intelligence. Bob, who was a silent, serious man, would sometimes squat beside him and talk in a low voice, and Jim began to brood, as much as it was his nature to brood, and to wonder more often what there was between Cooney and his old mate. But mateship forbade him to inquire. And so till cut-out, and next day, the river-boat being delayed, and time of little importance (for it was the end of the season), they decided to take the track up the river to the township where they intended to spend Christmas. As fuel to Jim's growing resentment, Cooney—who had a decent swag by this time, and a water-bag, thanks to Bob — seemed prepared to travel with them. Then Jim burst out

"——. it all Bob! Yer ain't going to take that—— on the track with us, are yer?"

"He's only going as far as the Wanaaring track," said Bob, "and then he's going to strike outback to look for a chance amongst the stragglers." Then he added in a mutter: "He's got pluck, anyhow, poor devil."

"Well I don't know about the pluck," said Jim, "but—why, he's got all the brands of a jail-bird or something, and I can't make out how in—— you came to cotton to him. I ain't goin' to ask neither, but if it goes much farther, it'll be a case of either him or me."

"You wait, Jim," said Bob quietly. "I've got my reasons, and I might tell you afterwards."

"Oh, orlright, I don't want to know."

They said little all day, except a word or two, now and again, with reference to matches, the direction, and the distance to water, for they were on the outside track from the river, and they were very quiet by the camp- fire, and turned in early. Cooney made his camp some distance from the fire, and Jim some distance from Bob—they lay as at the point of a triangle, as it happened; a common triangle of life.

Next day it was much the same, but that night, while Bob was walking up and down, as he often did, even after a long day's tramp, Jim, tired of silence, stretched himself, and said to the silent Cooney:

"Well, Cooney! What' yer got on your mind? Writin' poetry, eh? What's the trouble all this time, old horse?"

And Cooney answered quietly, and the reverse of offensively:

"Wotter yer care?"
"Wotyersay?"
"Whotter yer care?"
"W'yer say that for?"
"Oh, it's only a sayin'' I have."

That hopelessly widened the breach, if there could be said to have been a breach, between Jim and Cooney, and increased Jim's irritability towards his mate. But they were on the Wanaaring track, and next morning, after an early breakfast Cooney, who had rolled his swag at daylight took the track. He had the bulk of the tucker in his nosebag, for they would reach the township in the afternoon, and would not need it Bob walked along the track with him for a bit while Jim sulkily rolled up his swag. Jim saw the two men stop about half a mile away, and something passed between them, and he guessed it was a pound-note, possibly two, and maybe a stick, or so of tobacco. For a moment Bob stood with his hand on Cooney's shoulder, then they shook hands, and Cooney went on, and Bob came back to camp. He sat for a few minutes on his swag in front of the fire (for early mornings can be chilly outback, even in midsummer), and had another pint of tea to give zest to his morning pipe. He said nothing, but seemed very thoughtful.

"Well, Bob!" Jim blurted out at last "What the—— are yer thinkin' about?" Frettin' about yer new mate, hey?"

Bob stood up slowly and stood with his hands behind, looking down at the fire.

"Jim," he said, in his sadly quiet way, "that man and me was in jail together."

It brought Jim to his feet in an instant.

"Bob," he said, holding out his hand, "I'm sorry. I didn't know what I was drivin' at."

"It's all right, Jim," said Bob, with a quiet smile. "Don't say no more about it"

But Jim had driven to gold.

A friend or a chum might have shunned Bob after that a partner might have at least asked what he had been in trouble for; "a pal" would certainly have done so out of curiosity, and probably with rising admiration. But mateship didn't.

The faith of men is as strong as the sympathy between them, and perhaps the hardest thing on earth for a woman to kill.

Jim only glanced a little regretfully after the lonely little blur in the west and said:

"I'm sorry I didn't shake hands with the poor little ——. But it can't be helped now."

"Never mind," said Bob. "You might drop across him some day."

Such Is Life

"You're right, Thompson," said Cooper, at length. "Mostly everybody's got a curse on them. I got a curse on me. I got it through swearin' and Sabbath-breakin'. I've tried to knock off swearin' fifty dozen times, but I might as well try to fly. Last time I tried to knock it off was when I left Nyngan for Kenilworth, four months ago; but there happened to be a two-hundred-weight bag o'rice in the bottom o' the load; an' something tore her, an' she started leakin' through the cracks in the floor o' the wagon; an' I couldn't git at her no road, for there was seven ton on top of her; and' the blasted stuff it kep' dribble-dribble till you could a' tracked me at a gallop for over a hundred mile; an' me swearin' at it till I was black in the face; an' it always stopped dribbling' at night like as if it was to aggravate a man. If it hadn't been for that rice, I'd 'a' kep' from swearin' that trip; and' then, comin' down from Kenilworth with Thomspon, I'd 'a' kep' from it easy; for Thompson he never swears. I give him credit for that much."

TOM COLLINS (JOSEPH FURPHY)

THE BULLOCKIES' BALL

The team were camped along the gullies, Soon the news flew round about. Plans were worked out by Pat Scully, We gave the boys a grand blow-out We had an awning of tarpaulins, Kegs and casks came quickly rolling, Then the boys and girls came strolling To have a burst at the bullockies' ball.

On, my hearties, that was a party, help yourself, free gratis all Lots of prey and buckets of grog to swish away at the bullockies' ball.

First came Flash Joe, but Jimmy was flasher, Hopping Billy, the one eyed boss, Brisbane Sal and the Derwent Slasher Billy the Bull and Paddy the Hoss. Nanny the Rat the real May Cassa Brisbane Bess and Mother May Call, All come rolling together To have a burst at the bullockies' ball.

Soon pint pots began to rattle The cry was, "Pass the rum this way," The boys began to blow their cattle, The ladies, of course, must have their say. Sal said she'd take cheek from no man And Dawn to a dish of hash did stoop She'd got a smack in the eye with a doughboy Put her sitting in a bucket of soup.
Oh then boys, there was the ructions, Man the tucker and let fly, Brisbane Bess with a nunk of damper Caught Flash Joe right in the eye Nanny the Rat The real May Cassa With a frying pan a dozen slew She got a clip with a leg of mutton, Took a dive in a bucket of stew.

There was Wallowman Doughy Roly Foley, Said he'd put them to the rout, Seized a chuck of roly-poly Put a poultice of pigweed stopped his mouth This raised his old woman's dander And into an awful tantrum flew, "Fair paly" cried she to a bleeding overlander, "You pumpkin-peeling toe-rag coot!"

On, my hearties, that was a party, help yourself, free gratis all, Lots of prey and buckets of grog to swish away at the bullockies' ball.

A Cobb & Co. coach on the road.

Cobb & Co.

In its heyday Cobb and Co. was the largest single transport system in the world, running coaches throughout most of the settled rural districts of Australia. Freeman Cobb, a Californian, arrived in Melbourne in 1852 to look for gold, but he realised the need for a reliable system of transport to the Victorian goldfields and he imported coaches, harnesses and drivers to Australia. Cobb made a fortune in two years and sold out to a company of which James Rutherford, another American, was Managing Director, but the name Cobb and Co. was retained.

The company used Australian drivers intermingled with American experts. One of the characters among the Australians was Cabbagetree Ned Divine who drove the "Leviathan", a huge coach carrying 82 passengers which was drawn by 12 horses. There were other coaching services in Australia and some had started before Cobb and Co. It was the policy of Cobb and Co. to buy up its competitors and so it gradually got a stranglehold on the coaching trade.

One famous owner and coach driver who held out was Bill Maloney, who serviced the mining towns of Hill End, Sofala, and Tambaroora from Bathurst The fearless Maloney could always beat the Cobb and Co. coach along the narrow winding roads he knew so well. Eventually Cobb and Co. decided to relinquish its service in the Bathurst district and Rutherford made Bill Maloney a present of a new coach, "In appreciation for you being such a clean rival on the roads."

The Bullockies

Bullockies were the long-distance hauliers of the 19th century and with their yoked up bullock teams they could haul prodigious weights of goods—wool from the stations, wheat from the farms, timber from the forest, stone from quarries and all manner of goods. Like the long-distance truckies of today the bullockies were a proud breed of their own. They were tough, resourceful and capable of the most prolific streams of bad language as they urged their teams along.

There are many stories and not a few songs and poems about the bullockies in Australian folklore. Mary Gilmore in her book The Tilted Cart describes them as a superstitious lot "It was a common thing for teamsters to count their luck by a star. 'When I got to a certain tree and the star wasn't there I knew I would have bad luck,' I've heard more than one man say. One man came home to a sick child, unsurprised because no new moon had appeared above a certain tree at a certain bend of the road. 'I saw two shadows form a cross on the road, a real cross,' said another. From then on he camped every night early enough to read a chapter of the Bible before he turned in."

The bullockies were as much a part of the road in the 1 9th century as the ubiquitous sundowners but they were independent business men who took pride in their bullock wagon, looked after their teams and were expert at flicking a hide from their long handled whip over the backs of reluctant animals. So important was bullock transport in Australia that many of the country towns in eastern Australia are placed one day's bullock's drive apart The story of a bullock driver occurs in Joseph Furphy's Such is Life published in Sydney in 1903. Two well-known songs of the 1 9th century are The Bullockies' Ball and Bullocky-Oh! and a famous poem is Bullocky Bill

The Overlander

The strongest and perhaps most respected man of the bush was the overland drover — the man who brought great mobs of cattle from the stations down to market. The drover is pictured as a lean, tough, laconic figure who could sit on a horse all day and relax yarning with his fellows at night by a camp fire to ward off the cold of the inland, before turning in with the ground for a bed and a saddle for a pillow. He opened up the country as he found tracks with the best pasture and water for the mobs in his charge. He was the bushman supreme, resourceful, immune to hardship and dedicated to getting his cattle through, despite drought or flood or fire.

THE OVERLANDER

There's a trade you all know well,
It's bringing cattle over;
On every track to the Gulk and back
They know the Queensland drover.

Pass the billy round, my boys,
Don't let the pint pots stand there,
For to-night we'll drink the health
Of every Overlander.

Oh, I'm a bushman bold
Since youth I've been a rover;
On every track to the Gully and back
They know McVeigh the drover.

I come from northern plains
Where grass and girls is scanty,
Where the creeks run dry or ten feet high,
And it's either drought or plenty.

A girl in Sydney town
Said, "Please don't leave me lonely."
I said, "I'm sad but my old prad
Has room for one man only."

I never stole a shirt
As all my mates can say,
Unless I passed a town
Upon a washing day.

Cattle Duffers

In the days of the wide holdings of the squatter when cattle roamed on the free range it was comparatively easy for a cattle duffer to spirit a sizeable herd of beasts away from their owner, and hide them in a gully paddock or a small farm until it was time to sell them on the market. Cattle duffing was a widespread crime. Often herds were reduced along the way as a drover took his charges to market. One such cattle duffer was an Irishman named Devlin who owned a wine shanty at Overland Corner, near the border of New South Wales and South Australia. It was a secluded spot with green river flats hemmed in by cliffs, and cattle duffers brought stolen herds there and skinned them for their hides. While the drover enjoyed the hospitality of Devlin's shanty his men would steal some of the cattle and take them to a hiding place. The unfortunate driver might start the next day with a hundred or so cattle missing. When cattle stray in the area today the locals say, "Devlin's ghost took them!"

Making Do

Edward S. Sorenson in his book Life in the Australian Out Back Blocks paid tribute to the talent for improvisation of the Australian bushman. "The implements and appliances of the bushwhacker are in keeping with his surroundings. His rolling pin is a bottle: his toasting fork is made out of fencing wire: and his skimmer is a piece of perforated tin tacked on to a stick about two feet long. An old billy or pint Pot with holes punched in the bottom, makes a servicable colander: and the bread knife and carving knife are made from the broken blade of a hand saw, with two flat pieces of wood riveted on one end for a handle: his dishcloth is a piece of mole skin tied on the end of a stick and cut in strips . . . Iron hoop and fencing wire have a wonderful range in the matter of utility in the bush. So has green hide. This triumvirate figures in every hut and camp in the back country, and in the home or in the paddock it is the settler's ever lasting standby."

Rough Riders

The sport of Buck Jumping has been popular in country areas from early in the 19 th century and Australian rough riders are considered among the world's best. The first Australian rodeo with definite rules was held at Warwick, Queensland, and this is still the venue of the biggest annual Buck Jumping contest in Australia. Buck Jumpers who have become legends included Bobs, Gargin's Gray, Rocky Ned, Snips and Mandrake. Some say that Bobs, Gargin's Gray and Snips were never ridden for ten seconds, although Bobs was ridden by Lance Skuthorpe, best known of Australia's rough riders.

Other famous rough riders of the 1 890s were Carlie Steward and Harry "Breaker" Morant Skuthorpe toured America n 1938 and out-matched all riders that he met The modern rodeo which-derives from America and includes bull-dogging, steer roping and buck jumping, became popular after World War II.

Breaker Morant is remembered as one of the great figures of the Australian bush, and has had several books written about him and is the subject of a recently released film. Morant an Englishman, was a short story writer, poet, a boxer, stockman, and rough rider. He was the hero of countless stories of fantastic horsemanship. He enlisted in the forces for the Boer War in South Africa and spent six months leave in England in 1901. Returning to South Africa he joined the Bush Veld Carbineers which conducted irregular guerilla war with Boer outposts. Morant and another soldier, Handcock, were found guilty by the court and executed by the British Army for shooting several Boer prisoners, despite the fact that the Carbineers had orders to take no prisoners. Recommendations for mercy based on Morant's fine record, and the fact that one of the Boers who was shot was wearing a part of the uniform of a friend of Morant's who had been brutally murdered by Boers, were not upheld by the Tribunal. During the Court Martial Morant and those charged with him were released to aid the defence of a settlement against Boer attack. Despite appeals the sentence was upheld. Morant refused a blindfold and told the firing squad, "Shoot straight, don't make a mess of it." On the night before his execution he wrote a poem Butchered to "Make a Dutchman's Holiday."

A Fearful Track

The first cattle track in Australia is reputed to be the Murranji track which runs 140 miles from Newcastle Waters to Top Springs on Armstrong Creek, 8 miles from the farthest south out-station of Victoria River Downs. The track has claimed a number of deaths from thirst and fever.

Nathanial Buchan, when he formed Wavehill Station in 1883, pioneered this track for cattle travelling west Today the Marran-ji is a highway with water bores and tanks.

Ten, Ten, Two and Four

From the early days of settlement meat and flour, supplemented with tea, sugar and salt, were the staples of the colonial diet Convicts, servants and later labourers and station hands were paid in rations. usually 'ten, ten, two and four' that is 10 pounds of flour, 10 pounds of meat and 2 pounds of sugar together with a 1/4 pound of tea and 1/4 pound of salt The monotony of the diet and the poor conditions under which those 'forced to go on rations' worked and lived is told in this song:

THE OLD BARK HUT

Oh, my name is Bob the Swagman, and I'll have you understand,
I've had lots of ups and downs while travelling through the land
I once was fairly well to do but now that's all gone phut,
And I'm forced to go on rations in an old bark hut

CHORUS
In an old bark hut, in an old bark hut,
I'm forced to go on rations in an old bark hut

Ten pound of beef, ten pound of flour, some sugar and some tea,
That's all they feed a hungry man until the seventh day.
Unless you're mighty sparing boys you'll go with a hungry gut—
That's one of the great misfortunes in an old bark hut

CHORUS
In an old bark hut, in an old bark hut,
That's one of the great misfortunes in an old bark hut

The bucket I wash my feet in has to cook my tea and stew,
They'd say I was getting mighty flash if I should ask for two.
The table's just a sheet of bark, God knows when it was cut,
It was blown from off the rafters of the old bark hut

CHORUS In an old bark hut, in an old bark hut,
It was blown from off the rafters of the old bark hut.

On stormy days the rain comes in just like a perfect flood,
Especially through the big round hole where once the table stood.
It leaves me not a single place where I can lay me nut,
For the rain is sure to find me in the old bark hut.

CHORUS In the old bark hut, in the old bark hut,
For the rain is sure to find me in the old bark hut.

Of furniture there's no such thing was ever in the place,
Except the chair I sit upon and that's an old gin case.
I've a billy and a pint pot and a broken-handled cup.
And they all adorn the table in the old bark hut

CHORUS In the old bark hut in the old bark hut
And they all adorn the table in the old bark hut.

In summer when the weather's warm the hut is nice and cool,
You'll find the gentle breezes blowing in through every hole.
You can leave the old door open or you can leave it shut,
There's no fear of suffication in the old bark hut

CHORUS In the old bark hut in the old bark hut,
There's no fear of suffication in the old bark hut.

Beside the fire I lay me down wrapped up in two old rugs;
It doesn't make for comfort for it seems to lure the bugs.
And all I've got for company's me poor old collie pup.
So I use him for a pillow in the old bark hut

CHORUS
In the old bark hut in the old bark hut,
So I use him for a pillow in the old bark hut

And now I've sung my little song as nicely as I could.
I hope the ladies present didn't think my language rude.
And all you boys and girls around me growing up,
Remember Bob the swagman in his old bark hut

CHORUS
His old bark hut yes, his old bark hut
Remember Bob the swagman and his old bark hut

FIVE MILES FROM GUNDAGAI

I'm used to punchin' bullock-teams
Across the hills and plains,
I've teamed outback this forty years
In blazin' droughts and rains,
I've lived a heap of trouble down Without a bloomin' lie.
But I can't forget what happened me Five miles from Gundagai.

'Twas gettin' dark, the team got bogged, The axle snapped in two;
I lost me matches an' me pipe, So what was I to do?
The rain came on, 'twas bitter cold, And hungry too was I,
And the dog he sat in the tucker-box, Five miles from Gundagai.

Some blokes I know has stacks o' luck,
No matter 'ow they fall,
But there was I, Lord love a duck! No blasted luck at all.
I couldn't make a pot o' tea,
Nor get me trousers dry,
And the dog sat in the tucker-box, Five miles from Gundagai.

I can forgive the blinkin' team.
I can forgive the rain,
I can forgive the dark and cold, And go through it again,
I can forgive me rotten luck, But hang me till I die,
I can't forgive that bloody dog Five miles from Gundagai.

The Dying Stockman

A strapping young stockman lay dying, His saddle supporting his head; His two mates around him were crying, As he rose on his elbow and said:

CHORUS
"Wrap me up with my stockwhip and blanket, And bury me deep down below, Where the dingoes and crows can't molest me, In the shade where the coolibahs grow.

"Oh! had I the flight of the bronzewing, Far o'er the plains would I fly, Straight to the land of my childhood, And there would I lay down and die.

"Then cut down a couple of saplings, Place one at my head and my toe, Carve on them cross, stockwhip and saddle, To show there's a stockman below.

"Hark! there's the wail of a dingo, Watchful and weird—I must go, For it tolls the death-knell of the stockman From the gloom of the scrub down below.

"There's tea in the battered old billy; Place the panickins out in a row. And we'll drink to the next merry meeting In the place where all good fellows go.

"And oft in the shades of the twilight, When the soft winds are whispering low, And the darkening shadows are falling, Sometimes think of the stockman below.

Sundowners

As more people took to the bush in search of work a special language was developed to describe them. Sundowners were originally swaggies, drovers or shearers who arrived at sundown, too late to work but in time to seek a meal and shelter for the night The term has come to mean tramp.

The Billy

Perhaps the single most indispensable implement possessed by swagmen and bushmen alike was the 'billy'. There are several popular explanations for the origin of the name given to this handy cooking pot with a wire handle. One guess is that it is derived from 'billa' the Aboriginal word for water or perhaps from 'bally' the Scottish for milk pail.

Another theory is that the name comes from 'bully beef since the cans in which the beef came were often turned into cooking vessels. One other explanation is that the bush kettle had been called a 'royal George' during the reign of George IV and that after his death the slang became 'billy' after his successor King William.

On The Station

The Ringer

The ringer is a term which came to be applied to a champion shearer— one who scored the highest tally of sheep at a particular shed over a stipulated period. The all time champion shearer was Jack Howe who made a record with hand shears of 321 sheep in eight hours at Alice Downs Station in 1892. Another expression for the best shearer in the shed was "gun shearer". The expression has come to be applied to champions in other fields. Whenever a big gun shearer or a team of noted shearers were at work they attracted visitors from miles around, many with note books to keep a tally of the xcores. The song Click Go The Shears is surpassed only by Waltzing Matilda as Australia's best-known folk song, and depicts beautifully the bustle and competitive air of a big shearing shed.

CLICK GO THE SHEARS

Down by the catching pen the old shearer stands,
Clasping his shears in his thin bony hands.
Fixed is his gaze on a bare-bellied yoe,
Glory, if he get her, won't he make the ringer go.

CHORUS
Click go the shears, boys, click, click, click.
Wide is his blow and his hands move quick.
The ringer looks around and is beaten by a blow,
And curses the old snagger with the bare-bellied yoe.

In the middle of the floor in his cane-bottomed chair
Sits the boss of the board, with his eyes everywhere,
Noting well each fleece as it comes to the screen,
Paying strict attention that it's taken off clean.

CHORUS
Click go the shears, boys, click, click, click.
Wide is his blow and his hands move quick.
The ringer looks around and is beaten by a blow,
And curses the old snagger with the bare-bellied yoe.

The tar-boy is there and waiting on demand,
With his blackened tar-pot in his tarry hand.
Sees an old yoe with a cup upon her back.
This is what he's waiting for, "Tar here, Jack!"

CHORUS
Click go the shears, boys, click, click, click.
Wide is his blow and his hands move quick.
The ringer looks around and is beaten by a blow,
And curses the old snagger with the bare-bellied yoe.

The Colonial Experience Man, he's there, of course,
Shining boots and leggings, boys, just off his horse.
Casting round his eyes like a flaming connoisseur,
Shaving cream and brilliantine and smelling like a whore.

Click go the shears, boys, click, click, click.
Wide is his blow and his hands move quick.
The ringer looks around and is beaten by a blow,
And curses the old snagger with the bare-bellied yoe.

Shearing is all over and we've all got our cheques,
Roll up your swags, boys, we're off along the track.
The first pub we come to we'll all have a spree,
And everyone that comes along it's, "Have a drink with me!"

CHORUS
Click go the shears, boys, click, click, click.
Wide is his blow and his hands move quick.
The ringer looks around and is beaten by a blow,
And curses the old snagger with the bare-bellied yoe.

Down in the bar, the old shearer stands,
Grasping his glass in his thin bony hands.
Fixed is his gaze on a green-painted keg.
Glory, he'll get down on it before he stirs a leg.

CHORUS
Click go the shears, boys, click, click, click.
Wide is his blow and his hands move quick.
The ringer looks around and is beaten by a blow,
And curses the old snagger with the bare-bellied yoe.

There we leave him standing, shouting for all hands,
While all around him the other shearers stand.
His eyes are on the keg which now is lowering fast
He works hard, he drinks hard, and goes to hell at last.

CHORUS
Click go the shears, boys, click, click, click.
Wide is his blow and his hands move quick.
The ringer looks around and is beaten by a blow,
And curses the old snagger with the bare-bellied yoe.

Bush Fires

In the Australian summer the dried-out country lies under a constant threat of bush fires. After a series of hot dry days with north winds, a carelessly dropped cigarette or an unattended fire in the open can create an inferno which will sweep for miles across country. Perhaps the worst bush fire in Australian history occurred on Thursday, 6 February 18 5 1, which became known as Black Thursday. It was a day of 100° F with a howling north wind and bush fires raged over wide areas, described by some as stretching from the Dandenong Ranges in Victoria to Mount Gambier in South Australia.

A graphic description of a bush fire was penned by Marcus Clarke in his work Bush

Sketches. Black Friday which occurred on 13 January 1939 was more disastrous in terms of loss of life because the country was more settled. Seventy-one lives were lost on this day when strong winds fanned flames through forest country in many parts of Victoria. There was a magnificent response from the city to radio appeals for help. Volunteer fire fighters left the city in hundreds, transported by buses. The worst tragedy occurred at a timber mill where 15 of the 16 men who worked there were burnt to death.

A BUSH FIRE

It was my good or ill fortune to be present, only a fortnight back, at one of these terrible disasters. It was a hot afternoon in the Mallee scrub, and my host and I were smoking on the verandah, watching the eagle hawks float and pause in the cloudless blue sky, when T. suddenly started to his feet, rushed furiously to the rope of a big bell used by the cook to summon all hands to dinner, and fell to tolling it for dear life. I thought him mad, for nothing could I see in the direction to which his eyes were turned but a thin white column indistinctly outlined against the deep purple of the distant mountains. But others understood the action better than I. From the huts tumbled the men, all making for the stables, while, already through the swamp of the home paddock galloped the station horses, with the black boy, shouting and cracking his stockwhip incessantly in their rear. Such saddling and bridling was never seen since the days of Cannobie Lea.

"Come on." cried T. "It is a bush fire, and in the worst part of the scrub. Take any horse." In a few minutes we were all riding at break-neck speed through the bush, following the well-mounted T. as best we might, and stringing out like foxhunters. I found myself beside young Mr A, the second overseer, who was lighting his pipe a la Turpin as he. rode. "It is no use bursting our beasts." he said coolly. "That'll burn for many days before we can put it out." And he was right. How the fire originated no one knew, though there were wrathful suspicions as to one Sandy Joe, "a boundary rider", having fired the scrub to "get a burn", the said Joe being bigoted of opinion as to the value of burnt ground for sheep- feeding purposes but when we arrived it was raging into a sort of gully some 5O feet deep, choked with brushwood and blocked in the middle by a big rock, at which Sandy Joe was staring with an appearance of overwhelming interest. The thin column had now become a thick, dense cloud which must have been visible for miles, and the roaring of the flames almost drowned our voices. By T's directions the horses were put in charge of the least able of the party and secured in a sheltered spot on the weather side of the fire, while we, spread out in long line, went about half a mile on the lee side, and set fire to the grass there, beating out the fire again with long boughs, so that when the main body of flame reached the burned line it might have nothing left to feed on. But that fiery cohort came up, roaring in the tops of the trees, and was upon and past us almost before we could feel its heat leaping our little line without a pause, and flying away into the forest.

We had to run for our lives, and escaping danger of crushing branches, blazing bark, and sudden whirls of yellow fire, that would play and crackle about us from some sappy fern, fall with singed hair and blinded eyes into the company of our reinforcements. For the last two hours, it would seem, had neighbours been arriving —for all make common cause against the common enemy—but so furiously fierce had been the advance of the fire-flames, and so inextricably fixed were we in the dead waste and middle of it, that they could do nothing for us in that brief contest But now other arrangements were made. A boy was despatched for provisions and water cans. Spare horses were sent home.

We divided our forces, four or five to this spot, four or five to that. I was set to guard, if possible, a brush-fence, which if ignited would carry 30 miles of destruction along the mountain side. I said to my two mates—the prudent Mr A was in command of us —"How big do you think it is now?" "About four miles wide, I should say," said A., lighting the inevitable pipe with a bit of red-hot wood. I am told that it is characteristic of Australians to "blow". If I minutely described our night-watch in the hills I might be held accountant for as great a sin. The fire fought us inch by inch, and our brush fence had to go at last. Galloping some four miles to windward we tried again to "turn back on if ', and. after pulling down by main force half a mile of fence, thus "blowing up communication" (the brush-fence of Australia is made of trunks of trees drawn together by bullocks, and then interlaced with cut branches), we got the enemy turned away into the ranges. There he blazed for nine days until he got over the other side of the mountain, and we saw him no more.

During four days the fire lurked round us. The air was pungent with the aromatic odours of burnt gum leaves, the blackened branches and saplings striped our clothes as we walked, while the ashes lay ankle-deep on the black hot earth. At night the mountain gave out a dull light, while here and there along the range a burning tree would flame like a torch, and the embers of the red-hot stumps glow fiery red like danger lights. The birds had all gone. The kangaroo and cattle had fled. Even the dingos were afraid to pass that blackened and desolated forest

Poor T. lost 36 miles of fencing and 2,000 sheep which, being caught in the angle formed by the creek and the fire, were either smothered or burned. But on the tenth day after a big rain fell, and in less than a week all the burnt ground was green as emerald beneath the gray, dead trees. I came down to Melbourne with T. as soon as this happened, the richer by a strange experience in which the picturesque memories of the burning forest at night—one of the grandest sights in the world, believe me— blend strangely with recollections of burned hands and a longing for pure water unknown even to Sir Wilfrid Lawson.

MARCUS CLARKE

Famous Bells

On the station there have been some famous types of bells worn by cattle and horses alike so that stockmen and hutmen could keep trace of their charges. One was the Condamine bell. Mary Gilmore in her book The Tilted Cart, published in Sydney in 1925, said the first Condamine bell "was made from a pit saw-and in later years it was made from circular and from cross cut saws as well. Horses and cattle alike wore it and its note was so penetrating that in time it would render horses deaf As far as I recollect it, it had a hard steely sound something like a hammer clink on an anvil. In the sensitiveness of young years I was long haunted by the thought of how a horse suffered before deafness came as relief" Another famous bell was Mennicke's bell. Mary Gilmore mentions it in her poem Belts '11 Bullocks.

Once in a while we ask if he hears
The sound of Mennicke's bells
Deep in the pits of his ancient ears
Repeating their olden spells.
"Mennicke's bells,
Never heard none like 'em.
Mennicke he had the way,
No one else could strike 'em.

Mary Gilmore said in The Tilted Cart, "Mennicke was a blacksmith in north Wagga Wagga, New South Wales. He had a perfect ear for the sound of a bell. I remember hearing him tell my father that he imported his metals from Germany a rare and romantic thing in the seventies and eighties: and when he could not get it shipping (and teams from Sydney) being slow and uncertain, he would refuse to make inferior articles out of inferior materials. His bells were famous: they were small in size and of a tenor quality. One of my uncles told me once that he heard one six miles away on clear, frosty nights. Whatever other bells a teamster might have he always tried to have a Mennicke bell for the "straggler'. If ther were no straggler, Mennicke's bell went on "the leader". The Australian countryside once rang to the sound of cattle and horse bells and Adam Lindsay Gordon mentioned them in his poem Ye Weary Wayfarer.

Hark! the bells on distant cattle waft across the range,
Through the golden tufted wattle, music low and strange:
Like the marriage peel of fairies comes the tinkling sound,
More like chimes of sweet St Mary's on far English ground.

The Bangtail Muster

A bangtailed muster is usually held when a property is about to be sold so that an accurate account of the station's stock can be made. The brush of each animal is cut so that one would not be counted twice. A bangtailed muster was needed to verify the book muster and the number down on the station book was often far greater than the actual number on the run.

Cockatoos And Jackeroos

There are many likely sources for the expression "cockatoo farmer" or "cockie" which in modern parlance has come to be applied to anyone on the land but in past times has related to the small holding farmer as distinct from the squatter or large landowner. A "stringy bark cockatoo" was the poorest of farmers trying to survive on soil where only stringy bark gum trees would grow. A likely source of the expression comes from Henry Roberts in his book The Squatting Age in Australia published in 1935. "When he arrived at his destination if there was not a cleared space he had to make one." He would chop down a few trees so that there

The early dwellings of Australian pioneers were hand built on the site with whatever material was available Split timber, bark shingles. were common materials.

was room for a rough hut and some out-buildings, but usually other trees were ringbarked—that is, a circle was cut in the bark round trunks — so that they died. Eventually the trees fell before the winds and were cut up and dug out by the selector. But this process extended over many years. While they were standing, dead or dying, they gave shelter and food to myriads of grubs who lived under the bark. Flocks of screeching cockatoos came to feast on the grubs and so, it is said the aspiring farmers came to be known as "cockatoos" or"cockies".

The expression jackaroo was originally applied to a station apprentice usually of good family and sent from England for the toughening experience of outback life. It came to be applied to Australians of similar mould and the jackaroo system still operates in Australia. The name jackaroo is said to have begun in the Darling Downs of Queensland when a young Englishman named Jack Carew was engaged by a squatter as a "gentleman rouseabout'. A. B. "Banjo" Paterson described him in a footnote to one of his poems as "a young man who comes to a station to get experience. He occupies a position much like that of an apprentice on a ship and has to work with the men, though supposed to be above them in social status, hence the sneers at the jackaroo."

Calendar House

Mona Vale mansion, in the Tasmanian midlands, is popularly known as the Calendar House. So called because it was built in 1868 with 365 windows, 52 rooms, 12 chimneys and 7 entrances.

The Sick Stockrider

Sentimental tales of dying stockmen were common in the rhymes and ballads of Colonial times. The best known song goes:

Roll me up in my stockwhip and blanket
And bury me deep down below
Where the dingos and crows won't molest me
In the place where the Coolabahs grow.

The first poem to gain wide attention was Adam Lindsay Gordon's The Sick Stockrider included in his Bush Ballads and Galloping Rhymes of 1870.

THE SICK STOCK-RIDER

Hold hard, Ned! Lift me down once more, and lay me in the shade.
Old man, you've had your work cut out to guide
Both horses, and to hold me in the saddle when I swayed,
All through the hot, slow, sleepy, silent ride.

The dawn at "Moorabinda" was a mist-rack dull and dense,
The sun-rise was a sullen, sluggish lamp;
I was dozing in the gateway at Arbuthnot's bound'ry fence,
I was dreaming on the limestone cattle camp;

We crossed the creek at Carricksford, and sharply through the haze,
And suddenly the sun shot flaming forth;
To southward lay "Katawa", with the sand peaks all ablaze,
And the flushed fields of Glen Lomond lay to north.

Now westward winds the bridle-path that leads to Lindisfarm
And yonder looms the double-headed Bluff;
From the far side of the first hill, when the skies are clear and calm,
You can see Sylvester's woolshed fair enough.

Five miles we used to call it from our homestead to the place
Where the big tree spans the roadway like an arch;
'Twas here we ran the dingo down that gave us such a chase
Eight years ago — or was it nine? — last March.

'Twas merry in the glowing morn, among the gleaming grass,
To wander as we've wandered many a mile,
blow the cool tobacco cloud, and watch the white wreaths pass,
Sitting loosely in the saddle all the while.

'Twas merry 'mid the blackwoods, when we spied the station roofs,
To wheel the wild scrub cattle at the yard,
With a running fire of stock whips and a fiery run of hoofs
Oh! the hardest day was never then too hard!

Ay! we had a glorious gallop after"Starlight" and his gang,
When they bolted from Sylvester's on the flat;
How the sun-dried reed-beds crackled, now the flint-strewn ranges rang,
To the strokes of "Mountaineer" and "Acrobat".

Hard behind them in the timber, harder still across the heath,
Close beside them through the tea-tree scrub we dash'd;
And the golden-tinted fern leaves, how they rustled underneath;
And the honeysuckle osiers, how they crash'd!

We led the hunt throughout, Ned, on the chestnut and the grey,
And the troopers were three hundred yards behind,
While we emptied our six-shooters on the bushrangers at bay
In the creek with stunted box-trees for a blind!

There you grappled with the leader, man to man, and horse to horse,
And you roll'd together when the chestnut rear'd;
He blazed away and missed you in that shallow watercourse —
A narrow shave—his powder singed your beard!

In these hours when life is ebbing, how those days when life was young
Come back to us; how clearly I recall
Even the yarns Jack Hall invented, and the songs Jem Roper sung;
And where are now Jem Roper and Jack Hall?

Ay! nearly all our comrades of the old colonial school,
Our ancient boon companions, Ned, are gone;
Hard livers for the most part somewhat reckless as a rule,
It seems that you and I are left alone.

There was Hughes, who got in trouble through that business with the cards,
It matters little what became of him;
But a steer ripp'd up Macpherson in the Corraminta yards,
And Sullivan was drown'd at Sink-or-Swim;

And Mostyn — poor Frank Mostyn — died at last, a fearful wreck,
In the "horrors" at the Upper Wandinong,
And Carisbrooke, the rider, at the Horsefall broke his neck;
Faith! the wonder was he saved his neck so long!

All those days and nights we squandered at the Logans' in the glen
The Logans, man and wife, have long been dead.
Elsie's tallest girl seems taller than your little Elsie then;
And Ethel is a woman grown and wed.

I've had my share of pastime, and I've done my share of toil,
And life is short — the longest life a span;
I care not now to tarry for the corn or for the oil,
Or for wine that maketh glad the heart of man.

For good undone, and gifts misspent, and resolutions vain,
'Tis somewhat late to trouble.
This I know — I should live the same life over, if I had to live again;
And the chances are I go where most men go.

The deep blue skies wax dusky, and the tall green trees grow dim,
The sward beneath me seems to heave and fall;
And sickly, smoky shadows through the sleepy sunlight swim,
And on the very sun's face weave their pall.

Let me slumber in the hollow where the wattle blossoms wave,
With never stone or rail to fence my bed;
Should the sturdy station children pull the bushflowers on my grave,
I may chance to hear them romping overhead.

ADAM LINDSAY GORDON

The station owner and station hand of outback Australia, often of direct English extraction, had to rely on the infrequent arrival of the mail for his news of the outside world.

Belyando Spew

A sickness that was common among shearers and was marked by vomitting after meals was Belyando Spew, named after a river in Western Queensland. The illness was caused by the heat and the continual bending required in shearing work. A shearer's jingle refers to it.

On the far Barcoo where they eat nardoo,
Jumbuck giblets and pigweek stew,
Fever and ague and scurvy plague you
And the barcoo rot But the worst of the lot
Is the Belyando Spew.

The Rabbit Arrives

Australia has been infested with rabbits in plague proportions on a number of occasions in the past century. Although the disease myxomatosis, introduced by the C.S.I.R.O., has checked the progress of the rabbits, its influence has waned and rabbit numbers are again increasing. Wild rabits from England were liberated on Thomas Austin's property near Geelong in 185 9. It had become a pest within three years and within 20 it had reached New South Wales. By the end of the century the rabbit had crossed the Nulabor Plain and entered Western Australia, by-passing the 1,100 mile long fence that had been commenced by the Western Australian Government Professor Walter Murdoch has this to say on the arrival of the rabbit in an essay written in 1947:

The rabbit might be taken as a fine example of what we call patriotism. His supreme ethical motive is the expansion of the race. He dreams of the day when the rabbit family shall inherit the earth from pole to pole. If we would imagine a rabbit singing, we may suppose his song would be something like Rule, Britannia or Deutschlan uber Alles He is careless of the single life, the individual is nothing to him, the race is all. "Do what you will with me," he says 'trap me, poison me, skin me, pack me tight in tins, make my fur into a hat and my carcass into a pie — what does it matter so long as my race endures and spreads and burrows its way across kingdoms until all the earth is one huge rabbit-warren?" He is the perfect Imperialist— that however, is not my subject today; nor any other day. It deserves to be treated, not in my halting prose, but in Homeric verse. It is a matter for an epic. Mine is a humbler theme.

A little while ago you may have noticed on the cable page of your morning paper the following item: "The death is reported from London of Mr. John R. Collison of Maidstone, Kent who claimed to be the first person to introduce rabbits into Australia. He was 85 years of age." A few days later the cables informed us that ML Collison's claim to this distinction was disputed. Mr. C. J. Thatcher contends that his father was responsible for having introduced rabbits into Australia.

Now, to begin with, this conflict of claims is surely a somewhat curious and diverting spectacle. The idea of two men each "claiming" to have been the first to introduce a deadly pest into a country hitherto free from it has the charm of novelty. Mr. C. J. Thatcher, ready to die in the last ditch defending his father's claim to have done more harm to Australia than anybody else, presents a singular example of filial devotion. It is as if a man went about boasting that one of his ancestors had the honour of bringing malaria into Europe. It is as if a man gave himself airs because his Uncle Henry, and nobody else, had started the recent bushfires in Victoria. It is as if a statesman were to write a large book to prove that he, and he alone, had the honour of starting the Great War.

As to the historic fact, I have no doubt that Mr. C. J. Thatcher is in the right In 1863, or thereabout, some Victoria sportsmen, sighing like Alexander for more worlds to conquer, bethought them that the coursing of hares and rabbits was a luxury no civilized country ought to be without. So they applied to the Acclimatization Society; and the Society, thinking it rather a bright idea, wrote to its travelling agent in Great Britain, Mr. Manning Thatcher, who soon got together a sufficient herd of rabbbits and started for Australia in the sailing-ship Relief Ship. Life seems to have disagreed with the rabbits; when Mr. Thatcher reached Australia, not a single one of his rabbits was alive. But he, indomitable man, went straight back to England to get some more rabbits. His next attempt was again unsuccessful; and the next Three times he started for Australia with a cargo of rabbits three times he failed to bring a rabbit alive to port. Three times the gods strove to save Australia, but against determination like Mr. Thatcher's the very gods do battle in vain. On his third journey he had kept a close watch on his charges and found out the cause of their extraordinary death-rate; he provided a remedy, and his fourth voyage was entirely successful. It was as if the gods had given up the struggle in disgust; Mr. Thatcher landed without the loss of a rabbit

Meanwhile, owing to the long delay, the aforesaid sportsmen seem to have lost interest Mr. Thatcher found that nobody wanted his rabbits. With a companion, he went about the country offering baskets of live rabbits for sale, but he did not sell enough to pay expenses. His stocks of rabbits increased faster than he could sell them. One hot summer afternoon the two men decided that they had had enough of the tedious and unprofitable business; so they took all the rabbits out into the bush—and opened the baskets.

Some Advice on Rabbits

Federal Member, Winton Turnbull, often spoke on the rabbit menace and the shortage of wire netting. This prompted a letter from a listener dated 18 June 1949 from Callan Park, a large psychiatric hospital in Sydney.

Dear (Mr. Turnbull),

Many congratulations on the stand you have taken on the rabbit menace. Years ago they ate me out of a property I was on out West. Had a number of very dry seasons, no water and they ringbarked the few remaining trees, and as I was suffering from water on the knee, they eventually ringbarked me to get at the water. But did I give up the ghost?

No!—like a defeated politician I came again, full of the spirit of sacrifice. I went into another property and to beat the rabbit menace I introduced hundreds of oo-ah birds (pronounced oo-ah as though in pain). These are the only birds in the world that lay a square egg, during the process of which they scream and screech out oo-ah full blast. As they all lay at the same time the din is terrific. You just imagine it all square eggs coming out at the one time. It's colossal, it's stupendous. The rabbits can't stand the screaming and for miles around they flee the scene never to return while there are ooah birds there.

As there is a shortage of wire netting and the Opposition say the Prime Minister, Ben Chifley, is to blame for this, why not ask him to make available some of the ooah birds? Anyhow wire netting is no good to stop rabbits, as it is made up of thousands of little holes joined together, which eventually unite and make big holes so that rabbits get through.

I hope you will adopt this measure to combat the rabbit menace and so save this country for mallee roots and fat lambs.

I listen in to the Rumpus Room and enjoy the fun, but a few weeks ago it was hard to decide whether it was a private brawl or a free for all.

Now don't forget the oo-ah birds, the only birds in the world that lay a square egg.

Remember me to all the boys. Yours till the cows come home,

YOURS SINCERELY,
F.AT. LAMBS

Bush Expressions

The bush gave rise to thousands of words of slang and hundreds of delightful idiomatic expressions, no doubt delivered in a laconic manner in yarns over a drink or around a camp fire. The author of The Australian Language, the late Sydney J. Baker, gave these among a host of examples.

A man so short that to mount his horse he had to stand on his head to get his foot in the stirrup.

A sheep described by a shearer as having enough leather (loose skin) about his neck to make. say. dewlaps for a team of bullocks

Another sheep described by a shearer as having as many wrinkles in his hide as a concertina, or wrinkled from breech to breakfast time, or from afternoon to appetite, meaning in sailor's parlance from stem to stern; but the Australian bushman generally put his sayings stern first . . .

A snake longer than anyone can remember.

A long journey to an indefinite goal — a thousand miles the other side of sundown.

An aperture so small and tight that you couldn't drive a tin tack in it with a ton monkey.

Blankets so worn and devoid of nap that they wouldn't catch a burr if you dragged them from Bendigo to Bourke.

Anyone too slow to catch worms or to catch a cold, or to go to his own funeral or to get out of his own road

The average Australian has no better standard of speed than he's pretty sudden or swift or he can run (or jump) like a blanky kangaroo with a pot of horse blister stuck to his tail

From jackass to jackass is sometimes varied from jackass to mopoke— from dawn to dark.

Blood On The Wattle

The phrase "blood on the wattle" was used as an expression of rebellion against authority—of the need of the bushman, the miner, the working man, to fight against authority. It is based on a line in Henry Lawson's poem Freedom on the Wallaby 1891.

So we must fly a rebel flag As others did before us, And we must sing a rebel song and join in rebel chorus. We'll make the tyrants feel the sting O' those that they would throttle; They needn't say the fault is ours If blood should stain the wattle.

Bowyangs

A man on the track in early Australia wore bowyangs as a matter of habit. They were straps or strings around the trousers just below the knee cap and their purpose was to keep the weight of the trousers off the waist belt, or braces and make movement easier. Sidney J. Baker, in The Australian Language suggests that the term derives from the provincial English expression "bow yankies" which were leggings worn by agricultural labourers reaching from below the knee to the top of the boots.

Blue Stew

Alan Marshall, in Australasian Post. 18 February 1954, had a lovely tale to tell about a station cook:

"The Blue Stew Cook", a Darling identity, specialised in stew. He had a large, three legged pot into which mutton and vegetables were thrown each day. This regular addition to the stew meant that the pot always remained full. It simmered away above the fire from week to week, always retaining its volume, though a score of men were patiently eating it.

It was only natural that they began, finally, to look at the three-legged pot with some distaste. It was said that pieces of meat and vegetables lying round the bottom of the pot had been resting there for a month or more, despite the frequent stirrings to which the cook subjected the stew.

Finally, a dyspeptic shearer, determined to have the pot completely emptied for once, tossed a couple of knobs of Reckitt's Blue into it as he passed.

Just before the next meal the cook gave the stew its customary stir, started visibly, then recovered and yelled to the men as he ladled out the stew on to the waiting plates: "Blue stew to-day, boys."

Billy Tea

Billy tea is synonymous with life in the bush. It signals the start of each day and the welcome time of relaxation after mustering or shearing, or walking across country or droving, splitting logs in the forest, digging or fencing or working around the property.

Edward S. Sorensen in his Life in the Australian Back Blocks, published in 1911, had this to say, "Among some travellers billy boiling takes the form of a competition." A man of experience looking over an array of well-used billies says, "I'll back my billy to boil first" Interest thus being awakened, the others then put fiery spurts to their own utensils, each waiting, with tea bag in hand, for the first ripple. Of course, some are specially adapted for quick boiling, while others are "naturally slow". A man with a quick boiler is always ready to back it against any other. He understands it and can judge its boiling time to within a few seconds. An old billy will boil quicker than rain water, stagnant water quicker than running water, while water that has been once boiled and cooled will boil again quicker than any other.

The origin of the word "billy" is emphatically pronounced by the expert on Australian slang, the late Sydney J. Baker, as deriving from the Aboriginal word "billa", a creek or river. Three old expressions related to tea were: rationed tea, which meant poor quality tea included in station rations; post and rail tea, which was described this way because of pieces of stalk and leaf floating in it; and Jack the painter, a tea which left a stain around the drinker's mouth or in the billy. A substitute tea made in convict days from the leaves of the Correa plant became known as Botany Bay tea.

The Red Bull

It was not uncommon for dismissed workmen, aggrieved swagmen or itinerants who had been denied rations and shelter to set fire to a squatter's paddocks or to haystacks or outbuildings. The practice was known as "loosing the red bull", and the threat of it did a lot to ensure fair treatment from the hands of squatters for men who worked for them or those who came on to their property.

Up Country

Dorothea Mackellar became famous for our best known poem My Country a sincere, patriotic poem, it is known wherever there are Australians. Here is another Dorothea Mackellar poem Up Country which carries the same type of sentiment and has a familiar ring of metre and style.

Beyond the yellow levels,
The belt of dark belar
That edges the horizon,
There is a land afar.
A land of hope and promise,
A land of sweat and toil
A land of hidden waters,
And warm rich crumbling soil.

The burden of the summer,
That leaves the cracked earth bare,
Yet has no power to stifle
The life that slumbers there;
And, when the sky's hard splendour
Has changed to grey again,
The cool soft grey of rain-clouds
Low hanging to the plain.

And walls of rain close round
Then surely at our feet
The hidden life is stirring
To waken green and sweet.

And, if we have no autumn,
As people sometimes say,
And only very seldom
We know a winter's day—

(O, bitter wind of winter
That pierces to the bone!
We have no snow, but surely
A winter of our own)—
See how the sap is thrilling
In every growing thing!
They know not what they speak
Who say we have no spring.

Beyond the distant skyline,
(Now pansy-blue and clear),
We know a land is waiting,
A brown land, very dear.
A land of open spaces,
Gaunt forest, treeless plain:
And if we once have loved it
we must come back again

DOROTHEA MACKELLAR.

Brumbies

The word "brumby", to describe a wild horse, is said to have come from one Major Brumby who settled on a large grant of land at Richmond Hill in early Colonial days. He bred horses and a number of them wandered away from the property.When Major Brumby later left for Tasmania these horses could not be rounded up and became wild. Their descendants became known as brumbies.

A Squatter's Castle

A landmark of squatting times is Yulgilbar Castle on the banks of the Clarence River in New South Wales. The castle has more than 40 large rooms. The main building has an inner court and the walls of the towers are three feet thick. Workmen were brought out from England to build it by its owner, the Honourable Edward Ogilvy. Mr. Ogilvy kept a staff of liveried servants, a butler, coachmen and gardeners and his formal and correct household, who were all expected to dress for dinner, epitomised the aspirations of Australia's new squattocracy.

Yulgilbar Castle.

A Pommy Jackeroo

The jackeroo was often the butt of jokes and the subject of tall tales. The wayward sons of titled families were sometimes sent to Australia because few of their creditors would bother to pursue them to the other side of the world. Occasionally the young toffs could teach even an experienced bushman a thing or two as shown in this 1 920's incident related by Crane Rutledge.

Sometimes the Boss would send along a young man whom he had discovered, thinking he might be useful to me. Once an Englishman was sent from Toowoomba. He had beautiful clothes and spoke with a cultured voice but was not much use except for entertainment The other men would laugh at him behind his back, but not to his face. He always carried a compass which I admit I also found amusing.

Once a party of us were out surveying a bore drain on Fernlee. We had a horse and sulky to carry the gear and a couple of riding horses. There was the surveyor, the Englishman and another young man We had camped for three days and had finished the job late one evening, intending to go home the next morning. It started raining during the night and although we had pitched a tent most of us slept outside. I woke up in a pool of water. After a miserable breakfast we collected the horses, packed the gear and started for home. We were on lightly timbered box country; it was very cloudy with no sign of the sun. I rode ahead confident of my direction, expecting to find the gate in the boundary fence a few miles away, followed by the young man on horseback, then the sulky with the surveyor and the Englishman.

After about an hour I was well ahead and suddenly came on to fresh horse and wheel tracks in the mud. It took me only a few seconds to realise that they were our own. I turned back to Jack deciding to get a little amusement at his expense as he often boasted about his skill as a bushman. I said, "How do you think we are going? Do you reckon we are heading right for the gate?" When he replied, "Yes" I said, "Have a look at these tracks." He took some convincing but eventually had to admit that the tracks were our own. It was very easy to get lost and go around in a circle in flat country when the sun was hidden behind cloud. When the sulky came up, (it had been slow going in the mud) I sheepishly asked the Englishman if he had his compass. He cheerfully produced it and told me where north was.

How to Succeed

The suggestion of this unknown bush humourist, writing in the 1890s on a sheep station, could well be used as the Golden Rule for success by any young business executive today.

Dreamt other night I was appointed manager of " Dead Finish" station (owners

The Australian Broke and Reconstruction Co.) and received the following letter from the manager of the Company when I took charge, viz.:

PRIVATE

Dear Sir—you have been appointed manager of our "Dead Finish" station, at a salary of £100 per annum. I give these hints for your guidance and policy during your term of management viz.: I . Beware of "Big-head." 2. Write plenty of letters to the Company. Be as vague in your statements as possible, taking the Governor-General's speech to Parliament as a model. Fill your letters up with "Garden Stuff." The Directors have to make some semblance of earning their fees, and your letters will give them something to talk about at the "Board Meetings." 3. When you are asked for an estimate of "Receipts and Expenditure," don't write and say that it is all bosh and that not being Wragge you can't fortell a season, but make receipts as small and expenditure as big as possible. We may remember it at the end of' the year, and search for it in the dust-heap for comparison with results. If results are better than you prognosticated, the Directors will be pleased that through their efforts, they have done better than they thought they would do. If results aren't up to their estimate, you will have to take the blame. You are there for that purpose. You might write me a "private" letter, telling me what the station is really like. I can then tell the Directors what I think. I will add to my reputation, if it turns out as you say. 4. Do exactly as you are instructed by letter. Remember that the Directors and myself, with the help of sundry under-strappers in this office, and with some assistance from the London Board, are really managing the station. You are there to take

Henry Parkes, Esq. carried in triumph to the 'Empire' office.

the blame if any of us make mistakes. Directors don't like responsibility; neither do I. The Directors like all the credit. I like some, too, so there won't be much left for you. You are called "The Manager," that's your share.

5. Don't buy whisky and have it put down in the invoice as flour. If you get drunk, don't let me hear of it. I get a bit full at the club, with the Directors, at times but we are made of different clay. If I should come up to the station, we might get tight together, that won't count but it would be wiser for you to let me get drunk. Then you can attend to me while I am suffering a recovery.

6. Don't ask for a rise in salary. It might interfere with a rise I want myself. If you really want a rise, you had better come down and marry one of the daughters of our principal Director. I married one myself.

7. If you want "stud rams," write to the "Board." They will write to the London Directors, who always purchase the studs, knowing the least about it. If they turn out well (the stud rams, I mean), the "Board" will take all the credit If they are a failure, very likely you'll get the sack.

8. If you don't get dismissed for one of my mistakes, or for one of the Director's mistakes, or for showing that you know more than either of us. and become old in your service, or a blithering idiot from trying to do what a dozen people tell you about one thing, and if you haven't married our boss Director's daughter, we will most probably sack you and put a younger man in your place. Old beggars, as you will be then, should have saved enough money for their latter years. Finally, remember the importance of your position as Manager of one of this Company's stations (the Company has only reconstructed once). Entertain freely (at your own expense). The Company must be well represented. And do things handsomely (they want to float some more debenture stock) . Also, don't forget me. Tell everyone what a clever man I am. It might do me some good.

From Aboriginalities, 1890

A typical rural dwelling under construction.

SAID HANRAHAN

'We'll all be rooned,' said Hanrahan
In accents most forlorn
Outside the church ere Mass began
One frosty Sunday morn.

The congregation stood about
Coat-collars to the ears,
And talked of stock and crops and drought
As it had done for years

'It's lookin' crook,' said Daniel Croke;
'Bedad, it's cruke. me lad
For never since the banks went broke
Has seasons been so bad.'

'It's dry. all right' said young O'Neil,
With which astute remark
He squatted down upon his heel
And chewed a piece of bark.

And so around the chorus ran,
'It's keepin' dry, no doubt'
'We'll all be rooned' said Hanrahan,
'Before the year is out.

'The crops are done. ye'll have your work
To save one bag of grain;
From here way out to Back-o -Bourke
They're singin out for rain.

'They're singin' out for rain,' he said '
And all the tanks are dry.'
The congregation scratched its head
And gazed around the sky.

'There won't be grass, in any case,
Enough to feed an ass;
There's not a blade on Casey s place
As I came down to Mass.'

'If rain don't come this month,' said Dan,
And cleared his throat to speak—
'We'll all be rooned' said Hanrahan,
'If rain don't come this week.'

A heavy silence seemed to steal
On all at this remark;
And each man squatted on his heel,
And chewed a piece of bark.

'We want an inch of rain, we do,'
O'Neil observed at last;
But Croke 'maintained' we wanted two
To put the danger past

'If we don't get three inches, man,
Or four to break this drought
We'll all be rooned' said Hanrahan,
'Before the year is out.

In God's good time down came the rain;
And all the afternoon
On iron roof and window-pane
It drummed a homely tune.

And through the night it pattered still,
And lightsome, gladsome elves
On dripping spout and window-sill
Kept talking to themselves.

It pelted pelted all day long
A-singing at its work,
Till every heart took up the song
Way out to Back-o'-Bourke.

And every creek a banker ran,
And dams filled overtop;
'We'll all be rooned' said Hanrahan,
'If this rain doesn't stop.'

And stop it did in God's good time:
And spring came in to fold
A mangle o'er the hills sublime
Of green and pink and gold

And days went by on dancing feet
With harvest-hopes immense,
And laughing eyes behind the wheat
Nid-nodding oter the fence

And oh, the smiles on every face.
As happy lad and lass
Through grass knee-deep on Casey's place
Went riding down to Mass.

While round the church in clothes genteel
Discoursed the men of mark,
And each man squatted on his heel,
And chewed his piece of bark.

'There'll be bush fires for sure, me man,
There will, without a doubt.
We'll all be rooned,' said Hanrahan,
'Before the year is out

P. J. Hartigan

The Sporting Life

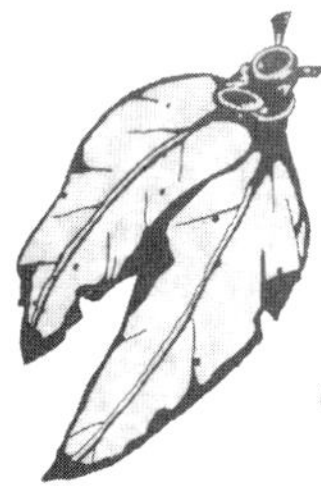

The Great Australian Game

Two-up is a gambling game believed to be unique to Australia. It is illegal, except under controlled conditions at the Wrest Point Casino in Hobart, and is therefore played well screened from the law in backrooms, lane ways, and secluded paddocks. It was extremely popular with Australian troops in both World Wars and is believed to have originated on the goldfields of Victoria. The story goes that a Frenchman saw Australian soldiers playing two-up shortly after they arrived in France in World War I. He exclaimed: "Never have I seen a people so devout. They gather in small groups along the water front. Then at a signal from the leader they raise their faces to heaven, only to humble themselves immediately by bending in the dust Mon Dieu, such devotion."

The game requires the simplest of equipment a flat board and three pennies. The players assemble in a room and one man, chosen or voluntary, takes the centre of the floor where he is given the kip, the small flat piece of board on which the pennies are placed for spinning. The spinner hands to the boxer, one of the organisers, the sum for which he wishes to spin and then goes about attempting to spin three heads in a row. Before spinning starts, side bets against the spinner are placed by watchers and they must equal the amount the spinner has wagered. When all is set there is a call from the ring keeper of "come in, spinner", and the spinner tosses the coins in the air. It is one of the fairest gambling games in the world as it is almost impossible to cheat.

Tub Races

Tub races were a highlight of Sydney's sporting events in the mid 19th century. They were held by fishermen who lived on the east side of Woolloomooloo Bay.

The tubs were large barrels cut in halves and with stools set into them on which the competitors sat as they sculled from the bay wharf, around Pinchgut Island and back. Pinchgut Island had its name changed to Fort Denison in 1857 in honour of the Governor of New South Wales. The island became a fort for the defence of Sydney in 1840. The Governor, Sir George Gipps, ordered the razing of its rocky formation almost to water level so that a fort could be built, but the project was abandoned until 1854 when Britain and France went to war with Russia. In 1857 the tower and guard rooms were finished and canons were pointing out to sea ready for use against invaders. The walls of the fort are 12 feet thick at the base and nine feet at the top and narrow stairs in the tower wind up to the gun room, where the 32 pound canons are still in position. The island was never used for the housing of prisoners as is popularly believed. The "dungeons" were used for the storage of powder and shot.

Cricket Record

An Australian team created a cricket record in being the first side to have an innings aggregate running into four figures. The Melbourne University Club scored a total of 1,094 while batting over four successive Saturday afternoons. Its hapless district cricket opponent Essendon could only manager to reply with 76 runs.

Emu hunting an early favourite sport.

Picnic Races

Picnic races are a great tradition in outback Australia — the means of people commuting from their far-flung properties for a taste of social life and lavish entertainment. The origin of picnic race meetings is believed to have been the result of a schoolboy pastime, when the Gibson and Chisholm boys built themselves a race track during the school holidays in 1830 and raced their ponies over the bush course at Goulburn. The races continued and as the boys grew up, Mrs. Gibson set aside special days for picnic races and issued invitations to her neighbours and friends in other districts. Guests arrived for lunch, and after the races, were entertained at a dinner or a ball at the homestead of the property Tirranna. The picnic races idea caught on in other parts of the State and then spread throughout the rural districts of Australia. Race activities may now be spread over a week in some of the more distant regions.

Betting Bowler

Among early Sydney cricketers the deputy Master of the Mint, Captain Ward, was prepared to back his skill with money. He was a left-handed, round-arm bowler and his critics said that he could be hit freely on the on side. Captain Ward offered £5 for every ball treated this way in a match and he bowled so well that he was later chosen for the Colony.

Victor Trumper Australia's great batsman.

The Great Trumper

Victor Trumper is considered to have been one of Australia's most accomplished batsmen. Although Don Bradman scored more runs and others had records to equal Trumper, he is considered by purists to have been a class above the rest in style and accomplishment. He played 40 Tests against England with a highest score of 185 not out and an average of 32.89. After passing the century he usually threw his wicket away. When chided by his captain, Joe Darling, Trumper said, "If I get a 100 and you chaps can't get the rest, you are a poor lot."

Trumper burst onto the scene in grade cricket with Paddington in 1896-97 when he scored 1,021 in 8 innings for 3 not outs and averaged 204 per innings. He scored 292 not out for New South Wales against Tasmania in 1898-99 and in the same season scored 253, in his last match of the season against New Zealand to win the individual aggregate score trophy for the season. He was selected to tour England in 1899, after a public outcry over his omission from the original selected team.

He failed in the first Test but scored 135 in the second and scored 300 not out against Sussex. Trumper's greatest season was on his third tour in 1902. It was one of the wetest seasons on record and Trumper proved himself on outstanding wet wicket batsman. His century before lunch at Manchester is classed as one of the greatest innings ever played. He scored a total of 11 centuries in first class matches on the tour. In 1902 playing for Paddington against Redfern in grade cricket Trumper scored 335 runs in 180 minutes. He hit 22 fives,39 fours and 37 singles, scored 32 runs from one over six balls and 50 runs in 51/4 minutes from ten balls

The poet Victor Daley penned these lines about Victor Trumper:

Ho statesman, patriot, bards make way!
Your fame has sunk to zero:
For Victor Trumper is today our one Australian hero.
High purpose glitters in his eye,
He scorns the filthy dollar, His splendid neck, says Mrs. Fry,
Is innocent of collar ...
Is there not happily, in the land some native borne Murillo to paint,
In colours rich and grand, This wielder of the willow?
Nay, rather let a statue be erected his renowned to,
That future citizens might see the Gods their sires bow down to.
Evo, evo, Trumper!
As for me it all ends with the moral that fame grows on the willow tree
And no more on the laurel."

Rorke's Drift

A Rugby League game between England and Australia in Sydney in 1914 became known as the Rorke's Drift Test after England battled through most of the second half with only ten men playing and still won 14-6. Rorke's Drift in Natal became a symbol of heroism in the face of overwhelming odds when 100 British soldiers held off an attacking force of 4,000 Zulu warriors.

The First Cricket Team Was Black

The first Australian cricket team to visit England in 1868 was called the Aboriginal Blacks of Australia. It was composed of Aborigines captained by the English cricketer, Charles Lawrence. The team played 43 matches in England—winning 14, losing 14 and drawing 15. Several country teams would not play against them, feeling that their dignity would be lowered, but they were invited to play at Lords by the MCC and were pitted against some of England's top performers. The Aborigines performed very well losing by only 55 runs. The outstanding member of the team was Johnnie Mullagh who later went on to play for Victoria in many matches. Another fine player was the bowler, Twopenny, who continued to play in New South Wales after the tour. Other members of the team were Bullocky, Redcap, Jim Crow, Mosquito, Dumas, Tiger, King Cole, Peter, Cozens, Charlie, Sundown, Shepherd and Dick-a-Dick. The severe climate played havoc with the Aborigines' health. King Cole died of pneumonia and Sundown and Jim Crow had to return to Australia before the tour was over.

The Demon

Frederick Robert Spofforth (1853-1926) was known as the Demon Bowler partly because of his devilish looks but mainly because of his fierce, determined and hostile attacks on the wickets of English batsmen. Spofforth took 767 wickets for 14 runs each in first class and his finest performance came at the Oval during the Australian cricket contest.

The Australians were skittled in the first innings for 63 and in turn dismissed the English for 101, with Spofforth taking seven for 46.

Then the "grand old man of English cricket", W. G. Grace, committed an act that had the Australians seething and turned them into an implacable fighting machine. The Australian captain Murdoch played a ball to leg and they ran a single. Lyttleton, the English wicket-keeper, ran after the ball and threw it back to W. G. Grace at the wicket. Play seemed over and the ball dead and Murdoch's partner S. P. Jones moved out of his crease to pad down the wicket. Grace whipped off the bails and appealed and Jones was given out.

After Australia had been dismissed for 122, Spofforth said to Grace, "By heaven you deserve to lose this match and by heaven you shall." Though England needed only 85 to win it was obvious that the Australians were going to try to mow their wickets down. Before taking the field Spofforth turned to his team mates and said: "This thing can be done." Spofforth took two early wickets with successive balls but Grace and Ulyett took England to 51 and the game appeared to have drifted away from Australia. However Spofforth changed ends with his bowling partner Boyle and, bowling with the dark pavilion behind him, delivered his fastest ball to Elliott, who snicked it to wicketkeeper Blackham. In the next over Boyle had Grace caught at mid off for 32—an innings described as "a masterpiece".

Spofforth and Boyle then delivered 12 successive maidens to the English batsmen Lucas and Lyttleton. Unable to break through Lucas's defence Spofforth spoke to Murdoch who agreed that Bannerman should misfield the next drive that came to him at mid of and concede a single that would give Lyttleton the strike. The concession was very extravagant for it was made when England, with six wickets still standing, needed only 19 to win. After delivering four maidens to Lyttleton, Spofforth got another ball through to the stumps. Four runs later he had Steele caught and bowled and two balls later he bowled Reid to have six of the seven wickets that had fallen. What has been described as "an awful silence" enveloped the ground. Through it, along the Vauxhall Road, came the clip clop of cab horses hoofs. During it a member was heard to remark, "If only they would play with straight bats they would be sure to get the runs", and his lady friend to reply "Would they really! Couldn't you get them some?"

Fred Spofforth Australia's demon bowler.

Then Lucas played on to Spofforth to make England 75 for eight, and a Lords member dropped down dead. Boyle's next ball had the Englishman Barnes. Now only the number 11, Peate, remained and he had three balls to face. He decided to attack two boundaries from him and one from his partner Stud, or better still three fours in succession from this over of Boyle's would have England home. Peate struck desperately at the first of the three balls and the batsmen ran two as it dropped close to the long leg fieldsman. He swung hard and hopefully at the next, but failed to make contact and was bowled.

Spofforth had delivered his last 11 overs for two runs and had taken four of the last six wickets. His figures for the innings were 28 overs, 15 maidens, 44 runs, seven wickets and for the match 64.3 overs, 33 maidens, 90 runs, 14 wickets. These figures have not been bettered by any Australian bowler.

In his autobiography Cricket W. G. Grace describes Spofforth thus: "His style has been described many times: right hand, a high delivery and fairly fast with a break from both sides, but chiefly from the off. Whether he broke 6 inches or 2 feet, so wonderful was his command of the ball that, if it beat the batsman, it invariably hit the wicket. His very fast ones were generally yorkers, which were delivered without any apparent alteration in pace. First class bowlers have come and gone with Australian elevens but to my mind not one of them has come up to the standard of Spofforth, who so rightly earned the name of the Demon, and never has a bowler fought more successfully or pluckily than he did that day of 1882 at Kennington Oval. The shouting and the cheering that followed his performance I shall remember to my dying day, as I shall remember the quick, hearty recognition over the length and breadth of the land that the best of Australian cricket was worthy of the highest position in the game."

The morning after that match the Sporting Times published its "in memoriam" notice which read:

In Affectionate Remembrance
of English Cricket
which died at the Oval
on 29th August 1882.
Deeply lamented by a large circle of sorrowing friends and acquaintances.
R.I.P.
N.B. the body will be cremated and the Ashes taken to Australia.

The Master

Herbert Henry "Dally" Messenger is recognised as perhaps the greatest Australian Rugby League player. He was known by team mates and fans as "The Master". His unpredictable running and astounding goal keeping so impressed English judges on the tour of the first Kangaroos team to England in 1908-9 that he was besieged with offers to join English Soccer Clubs. Tottenham Hotspur offered him £3,000. It is claimed that Messenger once leaped over a defender of an opposing team to score a try. In England he started behind his own line and ran the full length of the field to score a try.

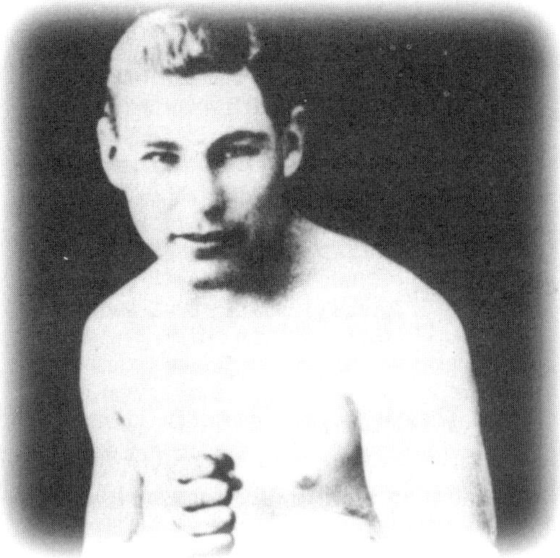

The Tragedy of Les Darcy

The great middleweight boxer Les Darcy (1895 - 1917) came to a tragic end far from home and reviled by the countrymen who had previously seen him as a hero. Darcy was born at Woodville near Maitland and was apprenticed to a farrier at the age of 16. He had his first professional boxing bout at West Maitland in August 1911 and from there went on to fight at Newtown and Sydney, defeating almost all opponents. His greatest triumph was over Eddy McGaughty, an American contender for the world mlddleweight championship, whom he thrashed in two separate encounters.

Fight promoters in America wanted Darcy and, although he had attempted to enlist in the army in 1916, he was frustrated by his parents' declaration of him as a minor. He defied the War Precautions Act and left Australia secretly, in October 1916, for America.

He was warmly greeted in the United States and was to be matched with Earl McCoy at Madison Square Gardens, but adulation died down as newspapers in America and Australia attacked him for not wearing an Australian soldier's uniform. He was branded as a shirker by the Sydney Sunday Times.

Barred from boxing in New York and in several American States, Darcy toured with a vaudeville troop. Finally the dispirited Australian champion took out US naturalisation papers and enlisted in the United States Air Force. He made plans to fight at Memphis, Tennessee, before going to war, but he was admitted to hospital suffering from septicaemia caused by infected teeth and aggravated by pneumonia. He died at Memphis on 24 May 1917. Darcy had fought in 44 major bouts for 40 wins, 20 by knock out.

Darcy's body was brought to Australia for burial and a crowd estimated at one million lined up to see him in an open coffin in a mortuary chamber at Woollahra, Sydney. His body was then taken to East Maitland where a vast gathering of mourners attended the funeral service. Father Cody, the priest officiating at the funeral said: "The doctor said he died of blood poisoning, the result of a complication of diseases. Those who loved him and knew him best and I am one of them, say he died of a broken heart."

Bare Knuckles

Larry Foley (1848-1917) was the greatest Australian bare knuckle fighter of his time. Foley, of Irish descent and a Catholic, defeated the Scot Sandy Ross, and a favourite of the local Orangemen, in a bare knuckle contest near Sydney in 1871. The fight was watched by enthusiastic supporters of the Green and the Orange. Foley was reputed never to have been beaten in ten years and his victims included the English champion Abe Hicken.

Popular Cheer

A popular song of the Australian Rules football season has made the expression "Up There Cazaly" a catch cry among the youngest football fans. They may not know that this was once a popular cry of encouragement in the 1920s which arose from the high marking skill of Roy Cazaly, who played with the South Melbourne team in the Victorian football league from 1921 to 1926. Melbourne rang with the cry for years and it became a battle cry of soldiers in the Middle East in World War II.

The Tied Test

Perhaps the most exciting finish ever in a game of cricket was the tied test between Australia and the West Indies at Brisbane in December 1960. Australia started the last over which was the last possible over of the match needing six runs with three wickets left The Australian Captain at the time, Richie Benaud, takes up the story from his book A Tale of Two Tests.

The game was tied with two balls to go! One run to win ... and the last man I(line joined Meckiff. Hall bounded in to bowl the second last ball of the match to Kline. He knew he must be deadly accurate ... The only way to prevent the batsman getting the run that would mean victory for Australia was to bowl at the stumps . . . To spread eagle them if possible.

There was not much sound on the ground at that moment and even less as Hall let the ball go, pitched in line with the middle and leg stumps, and Kline played it with the full face of the bat to forward square leg. The crowd screamed as the two batsmen set off on the winning runs. They crossed as Joe Solomon was just about to gather it in both hands .. . He picked up as Meckiff got to within about six yards of the safety of the crease. Solomon, the quiet one ... good and dependable ... the sort of man for a crisis. Was there ever a more crisis-like moment in a game of cricket than this?

There surely could never have been a better throw. The ball hit the stump from the side on with Meckiff scrambling desperately for the crease. Umpire Hoy's finger shot to the sky and there came a tremendous roar from the crowd of 4,000. .. who sounded like 20 times that number ... greeting the end of the game. A tie ... the first in test history.

Old Jack

Carbine is regarded as one of the greatest of Australian race horses. In winning the Melbourne Cup in 1890 Carbine or "Old Jack", as he was known, carried the weight of 10 stone 5 lbs and defeated 38 runners. No horse since has carried such a weight to victory and it was against the biggest field ever to run in a Melbourne Cup. The Aryus of the day reported "the thunder broke . . . the hill roared to the flat and the flat to stand and lawn. Hats went flying through the air like leaves rent by a September gale. Men leapt and shouted and women by the hundreds screamed with delight. Up in the wake of the horses flowed the people like flood waves across a barrier. All shouting, all cheering, all, whether they were winners or losers, full of exaltation over the greatest victory ever known on the Australian turf." In 1895 Carbine was sold for stud duty in England. For many years he stood at the property of the Duke of Portland, Welbeck Abbey. He sired the winners of 254 races. Carbine's skeleton is now at the Melbourne Museum along with the figure of Phar Lap, the only horse that could lay claim to eclipse Carbine's greatness.

The Golden Girl

Betty Cuthbert became known as Australia's Golden Girl after winning three gold medals at the Melbourne Olympic Games in 1956. The shy 19-year-old daughter of a New South Wales nurseryman ran with her mouth wide open as she streaked to victory in the 100 metres, the 200 metres and as the final leg runner in the 4 by 100 metres relay. She won the 400 metres event at the Tokyo Olympic Games in 1964 in the record time of 52 seconds.

Rules Invented

Australian Rules Football, which dominates winter sport in the four southern States, was invented by a New South Welshman, Thomas Wentworth Wills. Wills, who was captain of Rugby School in England, and who played cricket for Kent, returned home in 1856 and was critical of the lack of stamina of Australian cricketers. He decided that Rugby was too rough for Australia's hard ground. They evolved Australian Rules around a mixture of Rugby, Gaelic football and hurling. Wills was appointed Secretary of the Melbourne Cricket Club in 1858 and invited cricketers to play the game. The first reported match was between Melbourne Grammar School and Scots College in 1858. They played 40 a side with goal posts half a mile apart On three afternoons spread over a month, Scots was the only team to score in the first afternoon and the game was finally declared a draw.

The game was watched by a cousin of Wills, H. C. A. Harrison, and he and Wills modified the rules, notably placing the goal posts on a normal sized playing field. Harrison became the leader in the popularisation of the game which was gradually taken up by cricket clubs and schools.

The Barracker

The expression "barracking", meaning to cheer wildly for one's team or favourite in a sporting contest, was unique to Australia and perhaps the art has never been better developed than in this country where one-eyed barracking has become something of an art form. C. J. Dennis saw the one-eyed barracker this way:

I didn't want to see a game, nor see no justice done.
It never mattered wot occurred as long as my side won;
The other side was narks an' cows an' rotters to a man,
But mine was all reel bonzer chaps. I was a partisan.

Long Swims

Australians are very keen on endurance swimming. For 50 years a three mile swim in the Yarra attracted huge fields and another popular annual race has been from Magnetic Island to Townsville, a distance of five and a half miles, although swimmers must swim inside cages towed by boats to avoid shark attacks.

A famous endurance swimmer of earlier times was Annette Kellerman, born in Sydney in 1887. She swam in 20-mile races against men and made ten-mile swims in the Yarra in 1902. In 1904 she swam 17 miles in the River Thames and in 1906 she won a 23-mile race in the River Danube. She failed in three attempts on the English Channel.

Olympian Linda McGill became the first Australian swimmer to swim the English Channel in 1965 and she subsequently made two other Channel swims.

A lifesaver from Maroubra, Sydney, Des Renford, began a run to his series of Channel swims when he won a 37.6 mile swim down the Murray in 1969.

Surfing Illegal

Surfing was forbidden by law until a Sydney newspaper editor named William Gocher decided to defy the police. He advertised for three weeks in a row that he intended to defy the law and surf at noon on a Sunday. For two Sundays Gocher swam without incident but on the third one, as he buttoned a raincoat over his neck to knee costume, a police sergeant intercepted him and took him to meet the Police Commissioner in Sydney. Gocher pleaded for the freedom to surf without restriction and the Commissioner decided that police should not interfere with surfers at any time provided they were "properly" dressed.

How League Began

Rugby League in Australia began in 1907 after a dispute over the payment of expenses to injured Rugby Union players. Footballers who lost wages or even their jobs while absent through injuries met at the Sydney sports store of cricketer Victor Trumper to discuss their grievances. Sydney Club forward Alex Burdon broke his arm on a tour of the New South

Wales Northern Rivers District. He paid his own medical expenses and received no compensation for time lost at work. The players who met at Trumper's shop were incensed and they voted to quit Rugby Union and start a professional game guaranteeing players on tour ten shillings a day and seven and sixpence a day expenses. The move created a great split in Rugby ranks but gradually more and more players crossed over to Rugby League and it became established as the leading Rugby body.

The Red Terror

Phar Lap, Australia's most famous race horse, was known as the "Red Terror". He had 51 race starts and 37 wins, three seconds, two thirds and nine unplaced runs. He ran in three Melbourne Cups, finishing third in 1929, winning in 1930 and finishing eighth in 1931 when he carried the great weight of ten stone ten lbs. The chestnut gelding was ridden in most of his big wins by Jim Pike, and was taken to America in 1932, and won the Agua Caliente at his only American start Shortly afterwards he was poisoned in his box at Menlo Park, California, and his death plunged Australians into mourning for their great champion.

The First Skiers

In the 1850s miners from Norway strapped palings to their boots to ski on snowcovered slopes around the gold diggings at Kiandra, New South Wales. They used a single pole for balance and when they wanted to brake they put it between their legs and sat on it. Later they made skis from mountain ash. Some experts believe that skiing as a sport began at Kiandra. Tasmanian fur trappers fashioned shoe-like skis as early as the 1830s. After Kiandra's gold deposits were exhausted skis were only used by local farmers. With the erection of the Kosciusko Hotel and a chalet in 1909, and a chalet at Mount Buffalo, Victoria, in 1910, skiing began to become a popular pastime.

The Prince

John Macarthy Blackham was known as the Prince of Wicket Keepers. He visited England eight times and captained the Australian team twice. He invariably stood right up to the stumps to the fast bowling of the demon Frederick Spofforth and his partner, Henry Boyle. Catches behind were not so prevalent in those days as they are in modern cricket but in 28 test matches Blackham dismissed 46 batsmen,26 of them caught and 20 of them stumped.

The Greatest Day

Unquestionably Melbourne's most sporting day of the year is the Melbourne Cup. The entire country comes to a standstill at 2.40 p.m. on the first Tuesday in November to watch or to listen to the race and learn the fate of the millions of dollars that are bet with bookmakers or in lotteries and sweeps. The thousands of stories of the Cup begin with Archer who won the first two Melbourne Cup Races in 1861 and 1862. Archer, a big bay with massive hind quarters and a rolling gait that earned him the nickname of "the bull" became one of the few horses to win the Cup twice. Some others were Peter Pan, Rain Lover and Think Big, but outstanding champions who have won the race have been Carbine in 1890, Phar Lap in 1930 and Peter Pan in 1932 and 1934. Grand Flaneur who won in 1880 never lost a race. Bobby Lewis rode four Melbourne Cup winners and Darby Munro, W. H. McLoughlin and Jack Purtell each rode three Cup winners.

Referee Wins

A boxing referee scored a knock out in a fight in Sydney at the turn of the century. The fight was a match between Australian heavyweights Bill Turner and Bill Walsh and it became apparent early in the fight that Turner was trying to get into position to land a punch on the referee, Ernie Fullalove, without it appearing intentional. In the ninth round Turner hit Fullalove hard. Fullalove escorted Walsh to his corner and walked back to Turner who was standing with his hands at his sides and the referee crashed a right into Turner's face. Turner fell to the canvas and Fullalove walked back to Walsh and crowned him winner by a knock out.

Boxing Marathon

The longest boxing match held anywhere in the world with a duration of six hours 15 minutes took place at Fiery Creek, Daylesford, Victoria on 3 December 1856. The protagonists were James Kelly and Jonathan Smith. The first round lasted two hours under rules which ended rounds only when there was a knock down. Smith gave up in the seventeenth round. The two endured the marathon bare knuckle contest for a purse of £400.

Classic Fight

One of t he greatest and most exciting fights in the history of Australian boxing took place on 3 March 1947 when Tommy Burns, the welterweight champion of Australia, fought American negro, O'Neil Bell. Both fighters were tough hard punchers with great courage. They fought the first five rounds at a furious pace and by that time one side of Burns' face was swollen from temple to chin and his right eye had an inch-long gash above it. Over the next few rounds Bell tired slightly and Burns got in many telling blows but his hurt face was suffering with every blow Bell landed. Bell sprang to life in the ninth and they fought blow for blow until Burns crashed a right into Bell's left eye so that throughout the rest of the fight he was suffering a similar loss of vision to Burns.

In the middle of the tenth round Bell suddenly stepped away and then came forward. Burns met him with a left hook to the body and a terrific right to the jaw. Bell staggered back to his corner and Burns was on him with a fuselage of blows. Bell slumped to the floor and a huge cheer for the Australian favourite went up. However, it was too early. The referee, Joe Wallis, pointed to the electric clock above the ring. The bell had rung but no one had heard it. The next round began with Bell still dazed. He had gone only a yard or so when Burns delivered a series of well-placed blows that sent him reeling along the ropes and to the floor in a heap. Burns was crowned winner by a knock out. After the fight Burns went to bed for three days until the swelling on his face had subsided and he could see again through his bruised and swollen eyes.

Kangaroo Rocket

A great Australian cyclist in the era before Opperman was Jackie Clark who was known as the Kangaroo Rocket. He set many records at the height of his career between 1905 and 1920 and defeated visiting overseas champions in Australia and in America.

Cycling Phenomenon

Hubert Opperman, later to become Minister of Immigration in Australia's Federal Government, was a cycling phenomenon. He was Australian road cycling champion in 1924,1926,1927 and 1929. He held world records for 489 miles to I ,000 miles and his 24-hour world record, behind a pacer, of 860 miles and 367 yards set in Australia in 1932 remains unbeaten. In 1928 he won the French Bol d' Or, a 24-hour tandem paced event covering 565 miles, a record that has not been approached. He was voted the year's most popular sportsman among readers of the French newspaper Porto in 1931 after winning the Paris- Presse road race. He also won the world's longest nonstop road race—the 726 miles Paris-Brest-Paris event. In November 1937 he rode 2,751 miles from Fremantle to Sydney in 13 days, ten hours and 11 minutes.

Amazing Golf Record

Australia's most famous golfer, Peter Thompson, has won the British Open more than any other modern player, five times in 1954, '55, '56, '58 and 1967. Only Harry Vardon, six times, has won it more often than Thompson. Thompson was runner-up twice, in 1952 and 1953, before he won his first British Open and was runner up again in 1957. Thompson became the first player in the history of Australian golf to play five rounds under 70. In a tournament at Melbourne in 1959 his scores were 68,67,67,69 on a course rated as par 73.

The Million Dollar Mermaid

Annette Kellerman was Australia's first Champion Lady Swimmer'. She was born in 1887 and started training at the Cavill's pool in Farm Cove, Sydney, after she contracted poliomyelitis. By the age of fifteen she had set a number of record swimming times. In 1905 she toured Europe and established herself as a record-breaking endurance swimmer. Four years later Annette toured America giving swimming and diving displays and was soon appearing in spectacular motion pictures which included 'Neptune's Daughter' and 'Daughter of the Gods'. Annette set a women's world diving record when she dived 28 metres from a cliff for a scene in 'Neptune's Daughter'. She was voted the 'World's Perfect Woman' in the United States and in 1952 the film 'Million Dollar Mermaid' was made about her life.

A Nation of Swimmers

When all the obstacles to swimming on Australia's suburban beaches early this century are considered one wonders how on earth we managed to produce so many champion swimmers on our shores.

From as early as 1833 bathing was banned on public beaches in Australia between the hours of 6 am and 8 pm and the idea of mixed bathing was considered scandalous. Daylight bathing was first permitted at Manly Beach in 1903 although many swimmers had chosen to ignore the silly restrictions on bathing for some time before that. Mixed bathing was first permitted on Melbourne's beaches at South Melbourne in 1912 and was railed against by some as yet another decadent practice which like 'sunbathing', "a new form of idleness", was imported from Sydney.

The main cause of consternation for the officials was the "immodesty" of swimming costumes for both males and females. In 1907, by-laws in several Sydney municipalities required both men and women to wear a costume which covered their bodies from neck to knee, their arms from shoulder to elbow and screened their lower limbs from the hip to the bend in the knee with a skirt Such a garment was naturally very uncomfortable for swimming and the regulations, which also forbade swimming for periods longer than half an hour and sun bathing, met with very strong opposition from the swimming public. The laws were swept away nearly as soon as they were passed and a simple swimsuit of shorts to just above the knee with a sleeveless or short sleeved guernsey worn over the shorts to mid thigh, called the Canadian costume, became standard swimming attire for Australians.

The Australian Crawl

Dick Cavill, a fifteen year old from a family of swimming champions, is credited with developing the Australian Crawl and being the first to use the stroke in competitive swimming. When other swimmers commonly used the trudgeon stroke, young Dick developed a freestyle stroke with an independent kick which enabled him to vastly improve his speed through the water. In 1899 Cavill won the New South Wales 100 yards (91 metres) Championship using his new stroke. The name for the stroke is reported to have been coined when a runner-up in the race complained that he would not have Cavill "crawling" all over him.

Golf Arrives in Australia

The year 1882 saw the establishment of Australia's first golf club, "The Australian" in Sydney with links at Moore Park. Within a few years the club moved to Queens Park. In the years following clubs were founded at Brisbane, Melbourne and Adelaide. In 1894 the first Amateur championship in Australia was held, arranged jointly by the clubs in South Australia and New South Wales.

Troop Ships

Eighteen Foot Skiffs were first seen on Sydney Harbour in the 1890's but differed vastly from the gaily coloured speed machines that race across the harbour on weekends now.

Their heavy construction and the weight of old fashioned canvas sails and rigging meant that the skiffs had a maximum speed of only 12 km/hr. To increase speed 'on the downhill run' when sailing before the wind, the crews used to run up as many extra sails as possible. The resulting top-heavy rigs required the live weight of extra crew members to keep the little craft trimmed or balanced. As a consequence the early skiffs carried sixteen men crews earning them the derisive nickname "troopship".

Today the skiffs carry less than half the sail and with only three or sometimes two crew members average more than twice the speed and the slang "troopships" is now more correctly applied to the many crowded spectator craft which follow the race first around the course.

HOW McDOUGALL TOPPED THE SCORE

A peaceful spot is Piper's Flat The folk that live around—
They keep themselves by keeping sheep and turning up the ground;
But the climate is erratic, and the consequences are
The struggle with the elements is everlasting war.
We plough, and sow, and harrow—then sit down and pray for rain;
And then we all get flooded out and have to start again.
But the folk are now rejoicing as they never rejoiced before,
For we've played Molongo cricket and McDougall topped the score!

Molongo had a head on it, and challenged us to play
A single-innings match for lunch—the losing team to pay;
We were not great guns at cricket but we couldn't well say no,
So we all began to practise, and we let the reaping go.
We scoured the Flat for ten miles round to muster up our men,
But when the list was totalled we could only number ten.
Then up spoke big Tim Brady; he was always slow to speak,
And he said—'What price McDougall, who lives down at Cooper's Creek?'

So we sent for old McDougall, and he stated in reply
That he'd never played at cricket but he'd hall' a mind to try.
He couldn't come to practise—he was getting in his hay,
But he guessed he'd show the beggars from Molongo how to play.
Now, McDougall was a Schotchman, and a canny one at that
So he started in to practise with a paling for a bat
He got Mrs Mac to bowl to him, but she couldn't run at all,
So he trained his sheep-dog, Pincher, how to scout and fetch the ball.

Now, Pincher was no puppy; he was old, and worn, and grey;
But he understood McDougall, and—accustomed to obey—
When McDougall cried out 'Fetch it!' he would fetch it in a trice,
But until the word was 'Drop it!' he would grip it like a vice.
And each succeeding night they played until the light grew dim:
Sometimes McDougall struck the ball—sometimes the ball struck him.
Each time he struck, the ball would plough a furrow in the ground;
And when he missed, the impetus would turn him three times round.

The fatal day at last arrived—the day that was to see
Molongo bit the dust or Piper's Flat knocked up a tree!
Molongo's captain won the toss, and sent his men to bat
And they gave some leather-hunting to the men of Piper's Flat
When the ball sped where McDougall stood, firm planted in his track,
He shut his eyes, and turned him round, and stopped it with his back!
The highest score was twenty-two, the total sixty-six
When Brady sent a yorker down that scattered Johnson's sticks.

The Piper's Flat went in to bat for glory and renown,
But like the grass before the scythe, our wickets tumbled down.
'Nine wickets down, for seventeen, with fifty more to win!'
Our captain heaved a sigh, and sent McDougall in.
'Ten pounds to one you'll lose it!' cried a barracker from town;
But McDougall said, 'I'll tak' it mon!' and planted the money down.
Then he girded up his moleskins in a self-reliant style,
Threw off his hat and boots and faced the bowler with a smile.

He held the bat the wrong side out, and Johnson with a grin
Stepped lightly to the bowling crease, and sent a 'wobbler' in;
McDougall spooned it softly back, and Johnson waited there,
But McDougall crying 'Fetch it!' started running like a hare.
Molongo shouted 'Victory! He's out as sure as eggs,'
When Pincher started through the crowd, and ran through Johnson's legs.
He seized the ball like lightning then he ran behind a log.
And McDougall kept on running while Molongo chased the dog!

They chased him up, they chased him down, they chased him round, and then
He darted through the slip-rail as the scorer shouted 'Ten!'
McDougal puffed; Molongo swore; excitement was intense;
As the scorer marked down twenty, Pincher cleared a barbed-wire fence.
'Let us head him!' shrieked Molongo. 'Brain the mongrel with a bat!'
'Run it out! Good old McDougall! yelled the men of Piper's Flat
And McDougall kept on jogging, and then Pincher doubled back,
And the scorer counted 'Forty' as they raced across the track.

McDougall's legs were going fast, Molongo's breath was gone—
But still Molongo chased the dog—McDougall struggled on.
When the scorer shouted 'Fifty', then they knew the chase could cease;
And McDougall gasped out 'Drop it!' as he dropped within his crease.
Then Pincher dropped the ball, and as instinctively he knew
Discretion was the wiser plan, he disappeared from view;
And as Molongo's beaten men exhausted lay around
We raised McDougall shoulder-high, and bore him from the ground.

We bore him to McGinniss's where lunch was ready laid
And filled him up with whisky-punch, for which Molongo paid.
We drank his health in bumpers and we cheered him three times three,
And when Molongo got its breath Molongo joined the spree.
And the critics say they never saw a cricket match like that
When McDougall broke the record in the game at Piper's Flat
And the folk are jubilating at they never did before;
For we played Molongo cricket—and McDougall topped the score!

Thomas E. Spencer

Scenes from Australia-England test matches in 1894. The huge crowd gives an idea of the passion for the game. Of all the sports played in Australia, cricket aroused the most nationalistic feelings. Cricket was considered patriotic, enobling and uplifung. An article in the Australasian in 1872 touched on the character moulding qualities of the game in no uncertain terms: 'Let none grumble at the game he may deem "wasted" in frivolous amusement. Cricket is long past being an amusement only, it is more the school in which our youth are taught manly qualities of mind and body which will stand them, and perhaps their country, in good stead in after years.

Australians At War

The First Force

The first Australian soldiers emerged on 3 March 1885, when the country's first expeditionary force of 750 men left for the Sudan, marching through Sydney streets to the tune of The Girl I Left Behind. They took with them 200 horses and a six-gun battery in two troop ships. The raising of this Australian army was an emotional response to the news that the hero of the Sudan, General Gordon, had been trapped and killed. It turned out that the Australians were not really needed. They were involved in two skirmishes and a few were wounded. A member of the Sudan force, Private Robert Weir, of the 4th Infantry Company, was the first Australian soldier to die on active service. His death was caused by illness.

Emu Feathers

Tradition has it that the emu feathers in lighthorsemens' hats first appeared at the time of the shearers' strikes in 1891. Mounted riflemen from the Gimpie District were sent to help quell the disturbances and one of the troopers shot an emu and for decoration put some feathers in his hat. He looked so smart that the remainder of the troops followed his example and rode back to camp so adorned. The feathers were soon permanently adopted by the lighthorse regiment.

The Brisbane Line

The term Brisbane Line was derived from an allegation in 1942 that the Government had a defence policy which drew a line in an arc from Brisbane to Adelaide. Anything south of the line was to be defended by a concentration of military forces—north and west of the line was abandoned to the enemy. The allegations were made mainly by E. J. Ward, Minister for Labour and National Service in the Curtin Labor Government. He said that before his Government came to power in the early stages of war the line was part of defence policy. Ward's allegations led to the appointment of a Royal Commission and were a factor in the Curtin Government's decision to hold a general election in August 1943. The allegations created great controversy and bitterness among Queenslanders and Western Australians.

Short on Discipline

The Australian attitude to war and discipline began to emerge during the Boer War where a contingent of 3,000 soldiers joined British and other Commonwealth troops fighting there. The Captain of a Queensland unit was reprimanded by a British Officer for allowing his men to call him by his christian name, and for telling them the details of forthcoming action. The Queenslander replied, "I don't regard my men as private soldiers, sir. They are my mates. I want them to know why I am asking them to risk their lives."

Ice Cream War

The battle of Broken Hill took place on New Year's Day 1915, when 1,200 members of the Manchester Unity Order of Oddfellows and their families were aboard a train taking them to a picnic near Broken Hill. The train passed a deserted ice cream cart and at that moment the owner of the cart, a Turk named Good Mohammed, and another, Mullah Abdulla, opened fire on the crowd from nearby sand dunes. The motives of the Turks were mixed. They were resentful of treatment of them by some sections of the Broken Hill populus but they were also striking a feeble blow for Turkey's war efforts. The ice cream cart had a Turkish flag flying from a pole attached to it. Police from Broken Hill rushed to the scene of the battle, which claimed the lives of six people including the two Turks. Seven others were wounded. The incident led to the internment of all enemy nationals by the then Attorney-General, W. M. Hughes.

Chokkos Save Day

A battalion of young half-trained militia men known derisively as chocolate soldiers or "chokkos" stood between the Japanese and their intended conquest of Australia. When Japanese forces landed in New Guinea in July 1942 the 39th Battalion of Militia were the only troops available to rush to the Kokoda Trail, which runs between Buna and Port Moresby across the Owen Stanley Range. The raw and poorly equipped troops took on the Japanese on the mountainous muddy trail. In rain and mud, poorly supplied, and with no reserve to back them up, the chokkos disputed every foot of the jungle way. Superior forces and equipment eventually drove them back across the mountains from Kokoda, but their actions slowed the Japanese advance until the first transports of seasoned Australian troops reached Port Moresby from the Middle East. Although the veterans, too. were driven back at first, the Australian forces eventually gained ground and, using the jungle warfare tactics at which the Japanese were so adept, they beat the enemy at his own game. Their efforts led to the eventual defeat of the Japanese in New Guinea by American and Australian forces at Buna. The Australian defenders of Papua New Guinea were described as the Mice of Moresby by Tokyo radio because, said Tokyo, they spent all their time in their holes like their brothers, the Rats of Tobruk. They revelled in the name and a poem in the Moresby army news sheet retorted:

Rats of old Tobruk
Or merely Moresby mice—
We've had our share of fighting
And of hardships once or twice.
We have bugged the earth for cover
With the bombers overhead;
We have seen the bombs exploding,
Heard the swish of falling lead.
We have dived into the trenches
With our last remaining breath
Just a fraction of a second
Ahead of fire and din and death.
We have toiled and we have sweated
In the humid, tropic heat
And we've longed for many comforts
And fresh food that we could eat

But we'll grow our way to freedom
And we'll nibble at the scum.
Till we drive them back to Nippon
Or the hell where they belong.
And when they've learned their lesson
Then maybe, these foreign lice
Will remember "Rats of old Tobruk"
And Moresby's "Fighting Mice".

Furphies

The importable iron tanks used in military camps during World War I were supplied from a foundry established by John Furphy at Shepparton, Victoria. Camp rumours came to be known as "Furphies" and from its military beginnings the expression spread into popular use.

Fuzzy Wuzzy's

A popular name for Papua and New Guinea Islanders during the World War II was "fuzzy wuzzy". The stretcher bearers who became known for their care and patience with wounded soldiers during the New Guinea campaign were referred to as "fuzzy wuzzy" angels .

Monash's Greatness

An engineer and civilian soldier, Sir John Monash, led Australian forces to their greatest victory in World War I. Monash first won fame at Gallipoli as commander of the 4th Infantry Brigade and of the rear guard in the classic evacuation of the Peninsula. By 1918 he had commanded the First A.I.F. in France—five well-trained battle-hardened divisions. When the Germans launched their final offensive in 1918 the 3rd and 4th Australian divisions under Monash's command played a decisive part in holding the line. By August 1918 Monash had persuaded the Allied High Command to let him try his offensive tactics on a high scale. On 8 August the Australians broke through the German lines on the Somme and created a bridge which was never repaired by the Germans and ultimately led to their surrender; The German General Ludendorff later described 8 August as "Germany's blackest day". After the battle Sir John Monash was knighted in the field by King George V. Returning to civilian life he became Chairman of Victoria's State Electricity Commission.

Army Slang

Sidney J. Baker in his classic book The Australian Language points to the inventiveness of soldiers of the second A.I.F. in the use of slang and ribald expressions. The following examples are taken from his large glossary of expressions.

ANKLE BANGER, an overcoat.

BALLS UP, to make a muddle of A balls-up, a mess.

BATTLE BOWLER steel helmet

BATTLE BUGGY, used for a variety of vehicles in the desert

BLUDGE, to loaf.

A BLUDGE is the act of loafing; an organized BLUDGE is a BLUDGE engineered by a group or unit in a semi-official way. Also BLUDGER. "Come out you BLUDGERS!" a phrase used by Australians when routing Italians out of dugouts at Bardia and Tobruk.

BLUE, a fight a show.

BOOMERANG, it's a (or make it a), make sure that you give it back to me.

BORE IT UP THEM, to shoot at the enemy rapidly and effectively.

BREW UP, our army adopted BREW UP to mean that a tank burst into flames on being hit.

BROWNED OFF, bored stiff, fed up. Also bronzed off.

BUMPH, written or printed matter.

COCKY'S JOY, honey.

COMEDIAN, a commando, a disparaging name.

CRASH, a concentration of artillery fire.

GOLDFISH, tinned herrings.

GOOD HORSE, originally a good informant Later, 1943-5, a man of outstanding courage and fortitude.

GIGGLESUIT, fatigue dress. Also gigglehat gigglepants.

HAMMER INTO THE FLOOR LIKE A TACK, reprove, punish; a development of bash down.

HAVE THE GAME SEWN UP (or BY THE THROAT), to be master of, to know how.

HIT YOURSELF, to have a drink.

HOW'D HE BE! he's exceptionally lucky; also, he's a miserable opportunist. (at the expense of his mates).

HOW'S HIS DRF, how s his dirty rotten form!

IT'S NO GOOD FARTING AGAINST THUNDER, you're powerless against circumstances (or the authorities).
LADY BLAMEY, a beer bottle with the neck cut off, used as a drinking vessel.
MANDRAKE, a waterproof cape.
PALE VIEW, a dim view.
SNARLER, one whose services no longer were required by the Army, or SNLR. Only used to refer to soldiers returned from the Middle East on these grounds.
SWISH, A.W.O.L.
TROPPO, mad, referring (generally) to a person on whose nerves the tropics, the heat or the war (or a combination of these) are having an effect
WHAT'S IT TO YOU? mind your own business! (emphasis, strangely, on the word "to") .
WHIZZ IN, to come into an enterprise briskly, effectively.

From The Australian Language
by Sidney J. Baker (Sun Books).

Battle Of Brisbane

The so-called Battle of Brisbane occurred during 1943. It centred around the United States canteen at the corner of Creek and Adelaide Streets and was soon spread over a square mile of Brisbane city. One Australian died and seven Australians and eleven Americans were wounded during the battle, which involved brawling and some gun shots. The brawl was apparently caused because Australian servicemen resented the attention that the Americans were paying to Australian girls. Under constant enemy fire Simpson carried out this work for three weeks until he was killed by a piece of shrapnel on 19 May 1915. On his last day Simpson was making his way up from the beach when a cook called out to him, "Come and get your breakfast" Simpson replied, "I'll be back soon, keep it hot for me." A statue of Simpson and the donkey stands before the shrine of rememberance in the King's Domain Gardens in Melbourne. There is also a small bronze statue of him at the entrance to the Gallipoli Galleries at the Australian War Memorial in Canberra.

Arnott's Parrots

The emblem of the Sydney biscuit manufacturer, Arnotts, was a parrot on a perch chewing a biscuit. A long-standing joke from World War I relates how a defaulter from a desert base camp was subjected to a stormy ten-minute harangue by the base commander, one Colonel Arnott. The Colonel then asked him what he did in civilian life to which he replied: "Shot parrots for Arnotts biscuit tins."

The Anzac Book

The poems, stories and drawings by Australian troops at Gallipoli were collected into The Anzac Book, which was published in Australia in 1916. As the editor, the war historian, C. E. W. Bean, said: "Practically every word in it was written and every line drawn beneath the shelter of a waterproof sheet or of a roof of sandbags." Here is an example:

Corporal George L. Smith penned this cheerful little poem My Anzac Home during his short sojourn on the side of a hill at Gallipoli.

Come and see my little dug-out — way up on the hill it stands,
Where I can get a lovely view of Anzac's golden sands;
When "Beachy Bill" is shelling, I can see just where he lands,
From my cosy little dug-out on the hill.

It isn't quite as roomy as the mansions of the Tsar;
From sitting-room to bedroom is not so very far,
For the dining and the smoking-room you stay just where you are,
In my cosy little dug-out on the hill.

The fleas they wander nightly, as soon as I've undressed,
And after many weary hunts I've had to give them best
As the ants have also found it, there is very little rest
In my cosy little dug-out on the hill.

I've a natty little cupboard, and it looks so very nice,
'Twas made to keep my bread and jam, my bacon and my rice;
But now it's nothing other than a home for orphan'd mice,
In my cosy little dug-out on the hill.

There is no electric lighting in this blighted land of war,
So I use some fat in syrup tins, and stand it on the floor —
And when it's working overtime I sweat from every pore,
In my cosy little dug-out on the hill.

When the nights are clear and starry — then the scene is beautified
By the silvery gleams and shadows that across the mountain glide;
But if it's wet and stormy — well I go to sleep outside
Of my cosy little dug-out on the hill.*

When the time comes round for parting from my little eight by four,
And I can get a good night's rest without a back that's sore,
Well — perhaps some day I'll miss you, and will long to live once more
In the little cosy dug-out on the hill.

Corpl. George L Smith, 24th Sanitary Section, R.A.M.C.T.

The Anzacs

It is said that at Gallipoli Australia came of age as a nation. The prowess and the courage and the good spirit of the Australian fighting man in the appalling conditions on the Gallipoli Peninsula were praised by the British at the time and have become an enduring and proud part of the Australian legend. The British General, Sir Ian Hamilton, wrote the following lines about the Australians after he visited them at the bridgehead on 30 May 1915:

Men staggering under huge sides of frozen beef men struggling up cliffs with kerosene tins full of water; men digging; men cooking; men cardplaying in small dens scooped out from the banks of yellow clay—everyone wore a Bank Holiday air; evidently the ranklings and worries of mankind—miseries and concerns of the spirit —had fled the precincts of this valley. The Boss—the bill—the girl—envy, malice, hunger, hatred — had scooted away to the Antipodes. All the time, overhead, the shell and rifle bullets groaned and whined, touching just the same note of violent energy as was in evidence everywhere else. To understand that awful din, raise the eyes twenty- five degrees to the top of the cliff which closes in the tail end of the valley and you can see the Turkish hand-grenades bursting along the crest, just where an occasional bayonet flashes and figures hardly distinguishable from Mother Earth crouch in an irregular line. Or else they rise to fire and are silhouetted against the sky and then you recognize the naked athletes from the Antipodes and your heart goes into your mouth as a whole bunch of them dart forward suddenly, and as suddenly disappear. And the bomb shower stops dead—for the moment; but, all the time, from that fiery crest line which is Quinn's, there comes a slow constant trickle of wounded — some dragging themselves painfully along; others being carried along on stretchers. Bomb wounds all; a ceaseless silent stream of bandages and blood. Yet three out of four of "the boys" have grit left for a gay smile or a cheery little nod to their comrades, waiting their turn as they pass, pass, pass, down on their way to the sea.

There are poets and writers who see naught in war but carrion, filth, savagery and horror. The heroism of the rank and file makes no appeal. They refuse war the credit of being the only exercise in devotion on the large scale existing in this world. The superb moral victory over death leaves them cold. Each one to his taste. To me this is no valley of death — it is a valley brim full of life at its highest power. Men live through more in five minutes on that crest than they do in five years of Bendigo or Ballarat. Ask the brothers of these very fighters—Calgoorlie or Coolgardie miners— to do one quarter of the work and to run one hundredth the risk on a wages basis— instantly there would be a riot. But here — not a murmur, not a question; only a radiant force of comaraderie in action.

It was the physical appearance of the Dominion soldiers—Colonials as they were then called— that captivated everybody who came to Anzac, and there is hardly an account of the campaign which does not refer to it with admiration and even a kind of awe. "As a child," the novelist Compton Mackenzie wrote, "I used to pore for hours over those illustrations of Flaxman for Homer and Virgil which simulated the effect of ancient pottery. There was not one of those glorious young men I saw that day who might not himself have been Ajax or Diomed, Hector or Achilles. Their almost complete nudity, their tallness and majestic simplicity of line, their rose-brown flesh burnt by the sun and purged of all grossness by the ordeal through which they were passing, all these united to create something as near to absolute beauty as I shall hope ever to see in this world." Anzac Hymn

The Anzacs made up their own lyrics and sang them to the melodies of hallowed hymns, mocking their own heroics and appearance. To the tune of The Church's One Foundation they sang:

> We are the ragtime army,
> The A-N-Z-A-C,
> We cannot shoot we won't salute,
> What bloody good are we!
> And when we get to Berlin,
> The Kaiser he will say:
> 'Hock, Hock, Mein Gott!
> What an awful bloody lot
> Are the A-N-Z-A-C!'

Slouch Hat

In 1899 the Colonial Military Commandants agreed upon the adoption of the wide-brimmed bush hat for all forces other than artillery (who retained their British style sun helmets).

The first Australian unit to go into action, in the Boer War, Harry Chauvel's Queenslanders, wore their emu feathers in the fighting on I January 1900 (a year to the day before the Australian colonies formed a single Federation), and throughout the Boer War the Australians resisted British requests to replace their 'slouch hats' with regulation sun helmets the Victorians 'looped' theirs up on the right and wore a single eagle feather; the New South Welshmen pinned black cock's plumes to their hats.

The slouch hat, looped up on the left, embellished with the Rising Sun badge, was worn by Australian troops in two world wars and Korea, and became the symbol of the 'Digger'. When the Army changed into jungle green in the 1960s and rumours spread that the slouch hat would be discarded, public protest particularly in the Press, was such that all talk of replacing it ceased. It is, after all as Australian as the gum tree.

Jacka, VC

Members of the Australian forces were to win a total of 63 Victoria Crosses in the 'Great War' and lose 60,000 dead (a high cost for nationhood).

The first VC of the war became a legend. Albert Jacka, born near Geelong in 1893, was working with the Forestry Commission when he and two of his brothers enlisted in the First Australian Imperial Force. On the night of 19 May 1915, at Gallipoli he charged into a trench at Courtney's Post occupied by seven Turks and killed them, single-handed, securing this vital position in the Anzac line.

Commissioned (against his wishes), he became a national hero; his face appeared on recruiting posters. At Pozieres in 1916 a party of captured Australians suddenly saw an officer, firing a revolver, leading a group of men to their rescue. It was Jacka, now a lieutenant. Terribly wounded, he recovered and was awarded a Military Cross. Laying tapes on the night before Bullecourt in 1917 he ran into a two- man German patrol in the dark; when his revolver jammed he hurled himself at them and brought them in as prisoners. For this action— which many think deserved the award of a third VC — he received a bar to his MC.

Like many VC winners, Jacka was a paradox. He came from a family of strong Rechabite beliefs, he never touched alcohol and was embarrassed by popular acclaim. After the war he set up an electrical business, became Mayor of St. Kilda. The war had prematurely aged him and on his death in 1932 the city of Melbourne came to a standstill as a mark of respect.

Diggers

1917, the terrible year of the battles of Bullecourt and 'Third Ypres' saw the five Australian divisions, fighting alongside the New Zealand Division in two 'Anzac Corps', evolve into one of the most remarkable units under Haig's command. They had become an army within an army; and by the winter of 1917 the Australians had adopted the Kiwi expression 'Digger'. It remains the affectionate name for the Australian soldier to this day.

Britain, Canada and New Zealand (which was determined to maintain a fighting division in the field) had introduced conscription; the Australians twice rejected it in referendums and they remained, to the end of the war, the only all-volunteer force of the First World War. The Digger of legend had been born.

The British soldier was faced with the death penalty for desertion; the Anzac gaily went AWL or took 'French leave' whenever he felt like it, and maintained a running war with British Military Police. When a Redcap sergeant tried to break up a two-up game at Staples an Australian told him to 'go buzz off; when the troops at that bleak and ghastly training camp rioted in September 1917 Australians, Kiwis, Canadians and Scots led the mob, bashing up MPs and raiding the bars — in a similar riot in England, Australians were seen drinking pilfered beer out of fire-buckets. The British 'Tommy' was paid a shilling a day; the Australians remained the highest paid troops on the Western Front— 'The Six-Bob-a-Day Tourists' as they called themselves— and threw their money around liberally. Their general Birdwood, made a brave effort to make them salute and reduce their colourful language and then gave up. The Anzacs remained, to the end, blasphemous, profane, intolerant of discipline, riotous on leave, the most unforgettable soldiers the Western Front had seen.

'ANZAC' is Born

The first three Australian brigades made up the 1st Australian Division and the fourth brigade joined the New Zealand Infantry Brigade as the New Zealand and Australian Division. Together they formed the Australian and New Zealand Army Corps. It was a clumsy mouthful and before long storemen and clerks had abbreviated it to 'A.N.Z.A.C.' to save writing time and were soon using the initials on rubber stamps and stencils. ANZAC was also adopted as the code name for the force. Nobody would have foreseen that the word would enter the British language and that within months a small beach head would be called 'Anzac Cove', that fighting men of two nations would fight in France under the proud name of 'Anzac Corps' and that their valour would be commemorated annually on Anzac Day.

The 1st AIF

Within days of the declaration of war in 1914, a wave of patriotism swept Australia. "It is our baptism of fire," proclaimed the Sydney Morning Herald on August 6, the day that London cabled its grateful acceptance of Australia's offer to send 20,000 troops to aid the 'mother country'.

Thousands of volunteers rushed to enlist in the Australian Imperial Force for service overseas. Volunteers were aged between 19 and 38 and a minimum of five foot six inches (168 cm) tall. Men rejected for minor physical defects were heartbroken. Shearers, clerks lawyers and wharfies flocked to 'sign up' and all were happy to enlist as privates. Of the first 32,000 men who sailed only 7,000 were to return. The convoy departed from King George's Sound in November. En route its escort, HMAS Sydney left the ships, as they passed the Cocos Islands, to destroy the elusive German light cruiser, Emden, in Australia s first naval victory.

The excitement was shortlived. Camped in the desert near the Suez Canal, the Australians quickly grew tired of the delights of' Egypt. Enthusiastic, young and frustrated at being side-tracked to the Middle East while the battles raged in France, they began to earn a reputation for unruliness and lack of discipline that caused the British to believe that they would be of dubious value as a fighting force. In a notorious riot in the Wazzir district they burned down brothels and attacked natives. British troops were called out to restore order with fixed bayonets. The Australians drilled and trained in the desert but had ample leave to 'play up' in Cairo; in one incident some soldiers commandeered a train, threw the drivers off and drove it at break neck speed oblivious to the traffic signals. Other incidents included overturning vendor's street stalls, going absent without leave (one parade had to be called off because half the troops were AWL), and once some troops pushed their newly appointed commander off the pavement without saluting and pinched his staff car, which was found the next day near the pyramids. For all their swagger, noisy exuberance and lack of discipline the true spirit of the men, "You can't treat these fellows like regular soldiers," he once wrote.

The Western Front

When the first Australian divisions moved to the Western Front in 1916 one soldier wrote to a mate in Egypt that France was 'a picnic compared to Gallipoli.' The picnic was to end at a place called Fromelles in July 1916. Their first action was a 'diversion' to distract the Germans during the massive British offensive on the Somme. In the AIF's first major attack on the Western Front the 5th Division stormed the first two enemy trench lines and, their supporting division, the 61st British, having been unable to make any advance at all had to fight their way back to their lines at a cost of 5,533 casualties.

But Fromelles was just a prelude to the hell of Pozieres. Haig visited his Army commander, Gough, on 22 July 1916 to 'make sure the Australians had only been given a simple task.' The strongly defended ruins of the village had resisted British attacks during the slow advance and remained a dangerous salient bulging into the Allied lines. The 1st Division attacked it on 23 July; in four days over 5,000 of their men had fallen, destroyed by murderous machine-gun and artillery fire; by early September three Australian divisions had lost 23,000 killed and wounded, fighting through the rubble and mud of a place 'more densely sown with Australian sacrifice than any other place on earth.'

'The Somme' offensive continued until November 1916 when it died almost a natural death in a sea of mud. And with it died all dreams of the glory of war. For the first time Australians, usually laughing and joking even in the face of death, were seen trudging from the Line, grim, silent, dazed, 'like men who had been in Hell.'

And ahead lay two more years of fighting.

The Light Horse at Gallipoli

After three months of stalemate on Gallipoli General Sir Ian Hamilton was forwarded information that New Zealand scouting patrols had discovered that practically no Turkish posts could be found in the rugged country north of the Anzac beach head. This extraordinary news meant that the foreign campaign could-yet be saved: elaborate plans were made to land British divisions at Suvla Bay to link up with Anzac troops striking north, while at Anzac itself and at Cape Helles massive diversionary attacks would be launched against the entire Turkish line.

On the night of 6 August 1915 the New Zealanders moved off silently with fixed bayonets and without firing a shot—stormed and seized the high ground and by dawn had almost reached the crest of Sari Bair. In a matter of hours they had tripled the size of the Anzac beach head; it was a feat of arms that has few equals in the history of war.

General Birdwood now launched the Australians on frontal attacks against the Turkish trenches along the Anzac front, spearheaded by the Light Horse who had been rushed to the Peninsula to fight as infantry, and by the 1st Division against the 'impregnable' enemy defences at Lone Pine. At Lone Pine the Australians were to win no fewer than seven Victoria Crosses; they took the Turkish trench system and held it, suffering staggering losses. The Light Horsemen were to win no VCs but the sheer valour of their attacks in the face of point blank machine- gun fire remains one of the most incredible examples of the futility of war.

While the 1st Light Horse at Pope's and the 2nd Light Horse at Quinn's were slaughtered, the young Victorians and Western Australians of the 3rd Light Horse took up their positions in the trenches facing The Nek, a narrow saddle of land no larger than a tennis court. At 4.2 3 the naval bombardment suddenly ceased: the Navy had failed to synchronise watches, and for seven minutes of uncanny silence the dust cleared and the dazed Turkish defenders lining their trenches in double ranks, and well armed with machine-guns, prepared for the assault.

At 4 30 a.m. the first wave of Victorians leaped from their trenches and were cut to pieces in thirty seconds by Turkish bullets, before they had charged ten paces; at 4.33 the second line went forward and was mown down. Brazier, the commander of the third wave, pushed past his men who were already saying goodbye to their mates, for they knew they were facing certain death, and vainly sought a revision of orders. He was told that the attack must go forward. At 4.45 a.m. the third wave charged. 'With that regiment went the flower of the youth of Western Australia,' wrote Australia's war historian, Charles Edward Bean, with an emotion that surfaces rarely in his dispassionate and heartbreaking Official History, "sons of the old pioneering families, youngsters—in some cases two or three from the same home—who had flocked to Perth at the outbreak of war with their own horses and saddlery . . . Men known and popular, the best loved leaders in sport and work in the West . . . rushed straight to their death.'

Sickened by the needless carnage, Brazier sought out the Brigadier himself and demanded a change of plans. But the fourth wave were already filing into the trenches, fixing bayonets, resting their feet on the pegs, and an officer whose name has never been revealed asked them why they hadn't attacked. At 5.15 a.m. they went over the top into the hail of bullets. 'By God, I believe the right has gone!' an officer in the centre cried; and then the men on the left surged over the parapet.

Of the 600 men and boys of the 3rd Light Horse, 372 lay dead or wounded in the forlorn stretch of scrub of No Man's Land. It had been their first battle, and their last.

All the high hopes of a 'breakthrough' in August were dashed. The British divisions at Suvla Bay disembarked without encountering opposition and made no effort to strike south; when they finally mounted an offensive across the Salt Lake in September they were cut to pieces. In October Hamilton was replaced and the new Commander-in-Chief recommended evacuation of Suvla and Anzac. In December 1915, as blizzards heralding winter swept the Peninsula, the Anzacs were evacuated, leaving their 10,000 dead behind.

After Gallipoli all doubts about the fighting qualities of the Australian soldier disappeared. He remained the despair of 'spit and polish' British generals but his initiative, dash and courage won their admiration, and to Australians at home he became the idealisation of everything their men should be—brave, brash, cheeky, contemptuous of discipline, eternally cheerful.

Australian light horse on the last dash to capture Damascus, by artist H. S. Power.

The Navy

Australian sentiment for the navy has always been strong. It was the Royal Navy which first guarded our shores and charted our coastline, and was instrumental in ending the traffic in 'blackbirding' in the 1860's, apprehending the coasters carrying South Sea Islanders to work as slaves on the Queensland sugar plantations.

Before Federation the colonies had created their own naval forces. The old monitor 'Cerberus' can still be seen at Sandringham in Port Phillip Bay and the famous South Australian gunboat 'Protector' remains a rusting hulk at Heron Island.

The Commonwealth was the first dominion to form its own navy, against strong British Admiralty opposition. The Royal Australian Navy was formed in 1911 although the fleet did not arrive until 1913, on the eve of the Great War. Although the Australians saw little action in the first world war two submarines were lost.

The RAN

"The officers and men of these Australian destroyers out here are magnificent material and quite wasted in these old ships. Tovey has suggested that they might be transferred lock stock and barrel to five new ships and used at home. They certainly are the most lively and undefeated fellows that I have ever had to do with."

So wrote Admiral Sir Andrew Cunningham, Commander in Charge of the Mediterranean Fleet in April 1940, of the crews manning the 'Scrap Iron Flotilla' many of whom were reservists. The Commander's plans to transfer the men were never put into action since when Italy entered the war the Allied forces needed every available ship. Thus the Australians crewed these old ships— Stuart, Waterhen, Vampire, Vendetta and Voyager—until the end of the war.

Australians also manned the sleek new destroyers Napier, Nizam, Norman and Nestor; Quiberon, Quadrant, Queenborough, Quality and Quickmatch and the three Australian-built Tribals Arunta, Warramunga and Bataan in addition to the sloops and 60 corvettes built in Australian shipyards.

The 'glamour boys' on the five cruisers suffered heavily. Canberra, Sydney and Perth all went down in action; Hobart was torpedoed and Australia nearly destroyed by Kamekaze attacks. Churchill, moved by the staggering losses of the RAN made the Australian government an outright gift of the cruiser Shropshire in 1943.

Tobruk

On the 31 March 1941, sent by Hitler to retrieve the Axis fortunes in North Africa, struck suddenly at the thinly-held British front and four days later entered Benghazi. The only sizable holding force in the path of the Afrika Corps was Major-General Morshead's 9th Australian Division, newly arrived in the desert. Morshead had been asked to hold Tobruk for at least two months.

"There'll be no Dunkirk here," the general told his men. "There is to be no surrender and no retreat."

By April 11 the Australians had withdrawn into the town and were surrounded. Over the next three days they turned back heavy tank and infantry attacks even though they were subjected to constant bombardment by the German Stukas. During these first three days of the campaign Corporal J. H. Edmondson won Australia's first VC of the war.

The Unexplained

Birth Of The Bunyip

The Bunyip is a creature of Aboriginal legend which went by many names according to tribe and region, and came to be believed in and feared by white inhabitants of outlying regions. It was believed to live in the depths of lagoons and water holes, emerging on moonlit nights to catch and devour its luckless victims. It is said to have had a particular fondness for Aboriginal women. From their earliest contact with Aboriginals, Europeans began to hear tales of the Bunyip. Their descriptions of it varied but they were all in agreement in describing its bellowing voice and fiery eyes, its huge body, covered either by fur or feathers.

In the early days of Victoria, Governor La Trobe wrote that there were two kinds of Bunyip and he sent drawings of the southern kind to Tasmania, but they have now been lost There were various reports from eye witnesses. In 1872 at Narrandera, New South Wales, a Bunyip was seen by many observers and described as "about half as long again as an ordinary retriever dog, hair all over its body, jet black and shining. Its coat very long" In 1873 one was described from Dalby, Queensland: "It had a head like a seal, and a tail consisting of two fins, a larger and a smaller one." There were many witnesses in the 1870s to Bunyips in the Great Lake in Tasmania. One bumped a boat in 1873 and a Francis McPartland, in 1870, saw three or four together. The descriptions tally as a creature that was like a huge sheep dog about the head and from three to five feet long.

But the most fanciful description came from the Melbourne Morning Herald on 29 October 1849. "The veritable Bunyip has been seen at last! We are informed by Mr. Edwards, the managing clerk at the office of Messrs Moore and Chambers, that during his late trip, and making a circuit of Phillip Island, he and his party were astonished at observing an animal sitting upon a bank in a lake. The animal is described as being from six to seven feet long and in general appearance half man and half baboon.

"Five shots were fired and the last discharge was replied to by a spring into the air and a contemptuous fling out of the hind legs and a final disappearance in the placid waters of the lake. A somewhat long neck, feathered like an emu was the peculiar characteristic of the animal."

Ernestine Hill described a Bunyip which was reputed to have inhabited the Dynevor Lakes in South Western Queensland. "It is like a very large seal with a beard, they say, and no one can catch it, even when the lakes are low, but a postal inspector once gave me a photograph of it. He explained that while it showed up in the negative it never showed up in the print, which confirmed the general belief that it was a chimerical beast."

Ghost Stories

Australia does not have a great fund of ghost stories but a few have attained a national eminence through the continued retelling of ghastly tales.

Perhaps the best known Australian ghost is Fisher's ghost and it has greater credence than most as its supposed sighting led to the discovery of a body and a subsequent trial and conviction. Frederick Fisher, a convict who had received his freedom, disappeared in 1826 from his hut in the Campbelltown district. On 17 June 1826 John Farley, a ticket of leave man, rushed into the Plough Inn at Campbelltown and said he had seen the outlines of a ghostly figure sitting on a fence. He recognised the ghost as Fisher and as he approached, the figure pointed across a paddock towards a creek. Farley's story circulated in the town and came to the ears of the local police sergeant who decided to investigate. He sent a trooper and two Aboriginal trackers to the scene and they discovered dried blood on the fence. The trackers followed a trail toward the creek and they came upon the body of Fisher. Police investigations resulted in Fisher's partner, a man named Worrall, being charged with the crime. Though he professed innocence he was found guilty and sentenced to death. On the day of his execution he confessed to the crime. Campbelltown residents will tell you that if you go to Fisher' s farm about midnight on the night of 17 June you will see a dim figure leaning over the slip rails pointing in the direction of the creek that runs at the bottom of the farm.

Another well-known ghost in New South Wales is the Black Horse of Sutton. The horse was seen at intervals by a certain family but only when disaster befell their house. The first visitation took place when the father of the house went to Goulburn to arrange a land deal. As he was returning he was thrown from his horse and killed. That evening the man's wife was seated on the verandah of the homestead when she heard the echo of galloping hoofs along the home road. There was silence, then the sound of a gate being opened and the sound of galloping hoofs again. The woman stood up to welcome her husband, but a riderless horse came into view, its hoofs pounding on the drive. It crossed the lawn at breakneck speed and galloped straight towards the house but it vanished and the sound was muffled, only to be taken up again at the back of the house. When a search was made for her husband he was found dead, with his horse grazing nearby. The riderless spectre was seen galloping again, when the woman's eldest son was killed at the Boer War and again when he youngest son met his death in an accident.

Another ghastly sight is reputed to have been seen at Berrima, a beautiful Colonial town 100 miles south of Sydney. A woman named Lucretia Dunkley was hanged there. She was the licensee of the Three-Legs-O-Man Hotel, and convicted for murdering a wealthy farmer and robbing his corpse of 500 sovereigns. After her hanging her head was removed for scientific examination. Thereafter it is said that Lucretia's headless ghost began to roam the pine trees in front of the gaol. For decades sightings of her were reported but when the pine trees were cut down her haunting ended. However, as recently as Easter 1961 two youths camped near the ruins of the Three-Legs-O-Man heard sobbing efforts to breathe. They saw the headless spectre of Lucretia moving amid the ruins of her old hotel.

At Broome, the old pearling port of North Western Australia, there is a beacon on the foreshore that for no apparent reason sometimes becomes dim. Time and again the lights have been completely overhauled but to no avail. Without any known cause the light continues to grow dim as if enveloped by mist, even on the clearest of nights. The townsfolk believe that the ghosts of drowned pearlers flit and roam around the beacon on certain nights.

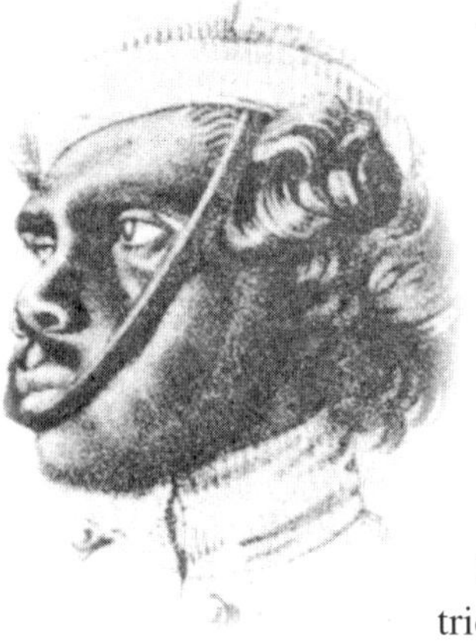

A native police tracker.

Every seven years on a moonlit night the ghost of Polly McQuinn appears at a waterhole known as Polly McQuinn's Waterhole in the Victorian district of Stathbogie. Polly McQuinn was a niece of Pollock McQuinn, a pioneer of the district. One day she went to Yarroweyah to buy household goods and the stream she had to cross rose whilst she was in Yarroweyah. When she returned the current was so strong that it swept her into the waterhole and she was never seen again.

Tasmania has a haunting on one of its most beautiful and famous landmarks, the Richmond Bridge. The mellow old freestone bridge, the oldest in Australia, was built by convicts. The story has it that they were overseen by a tyrannical foreman who aroused their bitter hatred. When the bridge was finished they murdered him and threw his body into the river. He is claimed to have been seen both in daylight and darkness, sometimes appearing as a man with a strange head dress and sometimes as a man with no head at all.

The ghost of Garth can be seen in a sinister stone building not far from Tingal in Tasmania. The house has never been lived in, nor was it ever finished by the workmen. Early in the last century a young settler, engaged to a girl in England, built the house for his future bride He sailed for England to bring her home before the house was completed but he found he had been jilted. On returning to Garth he hanged himself in the courtyard of the unfinished building. His ghost is said to haunt the place still. He had been joined by two other ghosts, that of a woman and a young child. The child fell down a well in the courtyard and a nurse was also drowned while trying to rescue her. Their graves are near the house.

Innaminka Crossing in Central Australia is the home of the ghost of Robert O'Hara Burke, the explorer who died of starvation at Quibidee Waterhole, after his base camp party abandoned it shortly before his return from the Gulf of Carpenteria. The grieving, wandering spirit of Burke may be seen alongside the tree marked with his initials, near where he died.

Discouragement: Burke, Wills and King arrive at Cooper's creek just hours after their relief party had left.

The Mystery Of Leichhardt

The disappearance of Ludwig Leichhardt one of the great figures of early inland exploration, remains, to this day, unexplained, though for a century bushmen have sought to find traces of his expedition.

Ludwig Leichhardt was born in 1813 in Prussia and attended universities gaining education in medical and natural science. He arrived in Sydney in 1842 imbued with the desire to explore the unknown inland. In 1843 he embarked on his first expedition inland and the following year ventured from Brisbane to the forlorn Northern Australian outpost of Port Essington. It was a nightmare of an expedition, but a triumph: he left the Darling Downs in October 1844 with four European colleagues (one of whom, John Gilbert was to be speared to death by natives), two Aborignes,17 horses and 16 bullocks. His party reached Essington in December 1845, returning to Sydney a national hero early in 1846, having completed a journey of 4800 kilometres in the searing heat of summer.

Leichhardt supported now by public donations, set off at the end of 1846 to cross the continent from east to west but had to return in failure, his party stricken by malaria, his qualities of leadership questioned. 'Why has my God forsaken me?' he cried.

In March 1848 he set off once again to cross the continent leaving Russell's station with a party of eight men including two Aborigine guides, 'Jimmy' and 'Billy', and 50 bullocks. In April he was pushing east from Fitzroy Downs. To a shepherd who asked his destination he replied: 'To the setting sun'. His expedition was never seen again.

Ludwig Leichhardt 1847.

Mysterious Disappearances

An unsolved mystery of the sea known as the Bermagui Mystery occurred in October 1880. A Sydney geologist Lamont Young and a German, Karl Schneider, were sent by the Mines Department of New South Wales to investigate a goldfield which had been discovered in the previous month. Young and Schneider had agreed to accompany three constables of the local police on a fishing expedition the next day, which was Sunday. Schneider returned to the geologist's camp and was never seen again. Young spent Saturday afternoon inspecting the goldfield and at 4 p.m. he met one of the constables who reminded him of the next day's fishing trip. He then set off for his camp and also vanished without apparent trace. When Young did not join the police party for their fishing trip they left without him. That same morning three fisherman from Batemans Bay took their boat out from a little inlet below the geologist's camp. These three men also vanished completely and their boat was found on Monday morning beached on some rocks about nine miles north of Bermagui. The boat had been deliberately holed by someone but it had remained afloat and opinion was that it had been steered ashore, not washed there. When police examined the boat they found many of the personal belongings of Schneider and Young. Several sacks of stones were also in the boat. The remains of a meal were found on the shore. Despite intensive police investigations no clues were found to the mystery.

A LEATHERWOOD PRESS BOOK

This revised edition of Treasury of Australian Folklore is published by
Leatherwood Press, 9 Watson Road Padstow NSW 2211

ISBN 186 5051 497

Distributed by Sandstone Publishing
Unit 1, 360 Norton Street Leichardt NSW 2040
Email: sasha @sandstonepublishing.com.au

Art and design by R BEE DESIGN
Unit 19/14 Frank Oliveri Drive Chipping Norton NSW 2170
Email: rbee@tpg.com.au

Printed in Malaysia

ACKNOWLEDGMENTS

The editors wish to thank the following authors, owners of copyrights and publishers who have given permission for the following material to appear in these pages. Hodder S Stoughton (Australia) Pty. Ltd. for the extract from A Tale of Two Tests by Richie Bernaud. Clancy of the Overfiow by A. B. Paterson reprinted from The Collected Verse of A. R Paterson by permission of the Copyright Owner and Angus and Robertson Publishers. The Australasian Post for the extract from Blue Stew Cook by Alan Marshall. Sun Books for the extract from From Curtin to Kerr by Fred Daly. The estate of Dorothea Mackellar for the poem Up Country. The Escape of the Fenians from Jack Loney's Maritime Australia. Currawong Press for the extracts from The Australian Language by Sidney J. Baker. Macmillan S Co. for the extract from In Search of Henry Lawson by Manning Clark. Hutchinson Group (Australia) Pty. Ltd. for the extract from The Lawyer Who Laughed by A S. Gillespie-Jones. For permission to reproduce photographs our thanks to the National Library of Australia, the Australian War Museum and the late Walter Stone.